Wealth Will Follow

Wealth Will Follow

Jeffrey Hair

CFI
Springville, Utah

ISBN 13: 978-1-59955-250-7

Published by CFI, an imprint of Cedar Fort, Inc., 2373 W. 700 S., Springville, UT 84663
Distributed by Cedar Fort, Inc., www.cedarfort.com

LIBRARY OF CONGRESS CATALOGING-IN-PUBLICATION DATA

Hair, Jeffrey Dale.
Wealth will follow / Jeffrey Dale Hair.
p. cm.
ISBN 978-1-59955-250-7
1. Finance, Personal—Religious aspects. 2. Wealth—Religious aspects. 3. Finance, Personal—Religious aspects—Mormon Church. 4. Wealth—Religious aspects—Mormon Church. I. Title.

HG179.H2325 2008
261.8'5--dc22

2008043660

Cover design by Angela Olsen
Cover design © 2009 by Lyle Mortimer
Edited and typeset by Heidi Doxey

Printed in the United States of America

10 9 8 7 6 5 4 3 2 1

Printed on acid-free paper

The unconditional love of my wife, Pamela, has taken me beyond the gravitational pull of this world; through her angelic ways I have experienced heaven on earth.

To her I dedicate this book.

Contents

"Mere words are cheap and plenty enough, but ideas that rouse and set multitudes thinking come as gold for the mines." —A. Owen Penny[1]

"There is one thing stronger than all the armies in the world, and that is an idea whose time has come." —Victor Hugo[2]

Introduction

Popular opinion holds that only a select few can enjoy the good life. The treasures in this book will prove otherwise. You are on an exciting threshold of a new beginning. Within these pages you will find an increased capacity for happiness, independence, and monetary success.

In just a few short years of effort and planning, my wife and I defied gravity and paid off our nice home, our automobiles, and all our toys. We are completely free of debt! At a time when foreclosures, bankruptcies, and financial crises are commonplace, our family enjoys the priceless commodity of peace. While freedom and choices continue to decrease for many, they are in abundance for us. We enjoy a lifestyle far above my rather ordinary income.

We would like to share with you twenty-one amazing treasures we were thrilled to discover along our unorthodox journey. These treasures have literally transformed our lives.

If you have the courage to implement them, the quality of your life will improve forever. So bid good-bye to the mistakes and heartbreak of the past; keep your eyes firmly fixed upon a whole new vision of what life is going to be. Fasten your seatbelts and hold on tight. You are in for an amazing ride to a brighter future.

Oh yes, as a cautionary note, I do not recommend reading this book under tall trees. The minute you cracked the cover of this book, you called down thunder—now get ready for the boom!

Notes

1. "A. Owen Penny quote," http://quotationsbook.com/quote/20148/
2. "Victor Hugo quotes," http://www.knowprose.com/node/13416

"So intimate is the alliance of mind and heart, that . . . the remedy for all blunders, the cure of blindness, the cure of crime, is love; . . . the redeemer and instructor of souls . . . is love." —*Ralph Waldo Emerson*[1]

Amazing Treasure Number One

Love: The Greatest of All Treasures

The mighty and wealthy "Solomon in all his glory was not arrayed like one of these" simple lillies (Matthew 6:29). Moses was taken on a visionary journey and permitted to see the earth, its inhabitants, and the ends thereof (Moses 1:7–8). Because the inhabitants were so numerous, Moses greatly marveled. After seeing you and me in our day, Moses said, "Now . . . I know that man is nothing, which thing I never had supposed" (Moses 1:10).

What would cause him to feel man was nothing? In a book by Karl F. Kuhn entitled, *In Quest of the Universe,* Kuhn reduces the galaxy to a manageable model. Here is an adaptation of his information:

> In this model the sun is diminished to the size of a basketball. On this scale, the earth is the size of the head of a pin, and its average distance from the sun is about 90 feet—about the size of a basketball court. The moon is about the size of a granule of salt, and is about three inches from the earth. Jupiter, the largest planet, is a large gumball about 150 yards away—1.5 football fields. Pluto, normally the farthest planet from the sun, is a grain of sand about seven-tenths of a mile away. Therefore, the entire solar system occupies an area a little over a mile in diameter with a basketball-size sun at the center.
>
> The nearest star to our model-sized solar system would be about 4,500 miles away. [If our sun were located in Salt Lake City the nearest star would be 2,400 miles beyond Hawaii.] This is about the average distance between stars in our Galaxy, so we must imagine millions of

> basketballs spread around randomly with approximately 4,500 miles between adjacent ones. The diameter of our galaxy on this scale would be about 1,000,000,000 miles.[2]

A few months ago, I read an article about a recently discovered galaxy that is estimated to be 100,000,000 light years from our solar system. The distance is almost incomprehensible. Just how many galaxies are freckled throughout the endless vacuum of space? Moses was overwhelmed when he was shown only the inhabitants of this earth.

To comprehend the vastness of the universe, I invite you on a journey through the endless regions of space. As we travel together, your assignment is to discover the most important law or principle of the universe. You will travel on a beam of light speeding through space at 186,000 miles a second. But in space even this speed is sluggish. Remember we just learned of a galaxy 100,000,000 light years from earth! On your trip you will learn about a variety of laws: Isaac Newton's theories on gravity, inertia, and motion; Albert Einstein's "General Theory of Relativity"; Niels Bohr's complex theories of the atom; and Johannes Kepler's "Laws of Planetary Motion." As you continue your voyage at light speed, these and other concepts will be laid out before you in simplicity.

At last, somewhere in the vast cosmos you will discover the principle you have been searching for. At first glance, it appears so insignificant you almost pass it by. At second glance, you are astounded by its intricacy and far-reaching ability to change lives. You are awed at the simplicity of its application. You see that by its influence lives are elevated and blessed. By its gentle power wars, evil, and hate are abolished. This principle has the power to uphold the entire universe and yet heal a single individual's soul. You have discovered the greatest act of love in the universe—the Atonement of Jesus Christ.

With this information in hand, you board the beam of light and speed toward home. During your million-year trip back to Earth, your eyes are opened to the profound purposes of life. You are able to look back upon the Pharisees and Sadducees, who clung to the law of Moses as if it alone would save them. Their harsh judging and rigidity caused them to be blind, but now you see with clarity—the one ingredient that was missing from their lives is the principle you have discovered.

Journeying on, you see the inhabitants of Earth in blind pursuit of material things, and, like Moses, you realize what makes man nothing—creatures only searching for gratification. As you near our solar system, you are awestruck at how closely it resembles a microscopic atom, and for a brief moment it appears that small. At length, our little planet (compared to the size of the head of a pin) comes into view and you begin to comprehend its micro-insignificance—a grain of sand in the dunes of space and eternity. From your present prospective, Earth appears so minuscule that you cannot see the American continent, much less the state or city where you live. This will cause you to ponder, "How substantial are my assets and possessions? How large is my home and property?" You realize those people who are caught up in materialism are exposed for what they are—nothing. As you come closer, you see a few people, here and there, who have lost themselves in the service of others and love of their fellowmen. Then a discovery bursts upon you: this is what turns the head of God—the pure love of Christ. Money is only a means to encouraging that love and so is everything else.

In one of the most hellish situations, Victor E. Frankl made a profound discovery. After spending years in Auschwitz; after being stripped of human dignity, honor, and the most basic of comforts; and after slowly starving and dying by degrees, he wrote, "A thought transfixed me: for the first time in my life I saw the truth as it is set into song by so many poets, proclaimed as the final wisdom by so many thinkers. The truth—that love is the ultimate and the highest goal to which man can aspire. Then I grasped the meaning of the greatest secret that human poetry and human thought and belief have to impart: *The salvation of man is through love and in love.*"[3]

It never ceases to amaze me that Frankl's discovery did not occur in some breathtaking setting, or at his mother's knee, but rather in the extreme circumstance of being surrounded by brutal human beings who constantly threatened him with extermination. Although his father, mother, brother, and wife died at the hand of his cruel captors, Frankl found supernal love in the gall of hell. Henry Drummond once said of the characteristics of love:

> Get these ingredients into your life. Then everything you do is eternal. It is worth doing. It is worth giving time to. . . . Address yourselves to that one thing; at any cost have this transcendent character exchanged for yours. . . . In the book of Matthew, where the judgment day is depicted for us in the imagery of One seated upon a throne and dividing the sheep from the goats, the test of a man then is not, "How have I believed?" but "How have I loved?" The test of religion, the final

> test of religion, is not religiousness, but love. . . . Not what I have done, not what I have believed, not what I have achieved, but how I have discharged the common charities of life.[3] (see Matthew 22:34–40)

According to Jesus, everything hangs upon the principle of love. Having been personally instructed by the Savior, Paul understood that love was paramount.

> Though I speak with the tongues of men and of angels, and have not charity, I am become as sounding brass, or a tinkling cymbal. And though I have the gift of prophecy, and understand all mysteries, and all knowledge; and though I have all faith, so that I could remove mountains, and have not charity, I am nothing. And though I bestow all my goods to feed the poor, and though I give my body to be burned, and have not charity, it profiteth me nothing. . . . And now abideth faith, hope, and charity, these three; but the greatest of these is charity. (1 Corinthians 13:1–3, 13)

Thanks to the teachings of Moroni, we understand that "charity is the pure love of Christ" (Moroni 7:47). Love is the gospel plan in a nutshell. John takes it one step further: "He that loveth not knoweth not God; for God is love. . . . And he that dwelleth in love dwelleth in God" (1 John 4:8, 16). So powerful is this principle of love that Jesus taught to "love much" would weigh in on our short comings.

> And he turned to the woman, and said unto Simon, Seest thou this woman? I entered into thine house, thou gavest me no water for my feet: but she hath washed my feet with tears, and wiped them with the hairs of her head. Thou gavest me no kiss: but this woman since the time I came in hath not ceased to kiss my feet. My head with oil thou didst not anoint: but this woman hath anointed my feet with ointment. Wherefore I say unto thee, Her sins, which are many, are forgiven; for she loved much: but to whom little is forgiven, the same loveth little. And he said unto her, Thy sins are forgiven. (Luke 7:44–48)

A pile of money sitting on a table has neither righteous nor evil tendencies. Isn't it the heart of man that determines whether money is good or evil? Is wealth pursued at the neglect of family, principles, and spirituality? Once obtained, is it hoarded? Is it used to bless the lives of others? Is it worshipped or used to elevate one above another? King Benjamin clearly understood the corruptive potential of wealth and gave up a life of royal comfort and privilege to work along the side of his people.

> But I am like as yourselves, subject to all manner of infirmities in body and mind; yet I have been chosen by this people, and consecrated by my father, and was suffered by the hand of the Lord that I should be a ruler and a king over this people; and have been kept and preserved by his matchless power, to serve you with all the might, mind and strength which the Lord hath granted unto me. I say unto you that . . . I have [spent] my days in your service, even up to this time, and have not sought gold nor silver nor any manner of riches [from] you. (Mosiah 2:13–12)

Moses surrendered his life of wealth and privilege in Egypt's royal family to answer God's call. A modern day Moses, the fearless Brigham Young was not afraid of the crushing persecutions or tribulations that faced the tender, growing Church. Although endowed with the courage of a lion, President Young feared the time when this people would become prosperous and wealthy. His experiences led him to warn,

> The Latter-day Saints who turn their attention to money-making soon become cold in their feelings toward the ordinances of the house of God. They neglect their prayers, become unwilling to pay any donations; the law of Tithing gets too great a task for them; and they finally forsake their God, and the providences of heaven seem to be shut out from them—all in consequence of this lust after the things of this world, which will certainly perish in handling, and in their use they will fade away and go from us.[5]

One of the most profound and repeated messages of the Book of Mormon is human beings' struggle with pride and wealth. Apparently, if we're not plagued with disease; or busy running from the imminence of our enemy's sword, daily fearful for our lives; or unless we're without food, slowly starving to death, we become prideful and forget God.

> And thus we see that except the Lord doth chasten his people with many afflictions, yea, except he doth visit them with death and with terror, and with famine and with all manner of pestilence, they will not remember him. Oh how foolish, and how vain, and how evil, and devilish, and how quick to do iniquity, and how slow to do good, are the children of men; yea, how quick to hearken unto the words of the evil one, and to set their hearts upon the vain things of the world! Yea how quick to be lifted up in pride; yea, how quick to boast, and do all manner of that which is iniquity . . . yea, how slow to walk in wisdom's path! . . . Oh how great is the nothingness of the children

of men. (Helaman 12:3–5, 7)

Seeking answers through the fog of today's disintegrating morals, where righteousness is seen as antiquated and foolish, and sin as inviting and desirable, discovering God's will may not be such an easy task. If we are to avoid the mistakes of our Book of Mormon counterparts, we must truly hunger and thirst to do His will daily.

Late one evening I assisted an ailing friend into bed. This gentleman had enjoyed a distinguished career and served this nation at high levels, but age and the seemingly endless rigors of his positions had finally taken their toll on his health. Now, behind closed doors, he quietly struggled with growing physical frailties and the painful awareness he could no longer shoulder such heavy loads. He understood the nation would need to move forward without him. Soon through death he would pass the symbolic torch on to a younger generation, who, I found myself hoping and praying, would follow in his statesman-like footsteps.

As I sat at the bedside, to help break the monotony, I asked my frail, old friend if he were given the opportunity to address the people again what he would say. The thought brought a smile to his face. He looked up at me and deep emotion overcame him. I felt I understood and attempted to comfort him. This man learned to love the people he served in various capacities of leadership throughout his life and desperately did not want to leave them. But he knew the signs of dying all to well. During his lifetime he had watched men go through the same declining process. He fully understood that he would never again address the public. Holding his hands and standing at his bedside I choked back my own emotions and continued, "Would you talk about the evils of communism, sir?"

Still emotional and somewhat preoccupied he said, "No."

"Would you talk about the great land of America, a land choice above all other lands, or perhaps the divinely inspired Constitution?"

Again, he said, "No."

I tried other questions and received the same response. "Then tell me," I continued, "what would you tell this people?"

He looked up and gently grabbed my arm. His smile faded. With concern on his face and desperation in his voice, and with a degree of physical difficulty, he uttered thirteen profound, yet simple words, "I would tell them to love one another and stop all this nonsense." He then smiled longingly, and shook his head as tears filled his eyes.

"That was the most beautiful sermon I have ever heard," I said, as I hugged him good night. How these words have touched my life. At the twilight of his life, having served in the inner circle of the most powerful government on the planet, he uttered the most profound five-second message I had ever heard.

President Benson once said, "When we put God first, all other things fall into their proper place or drop out of our lives. Our love of the Lord will govern the claims for our affection, the demands on our time, the interests we pursue, and the order of our priorities."[6]

If we can come to an understanding of this principle as taught by Jesus Christ, and then live it, we will find the happiness that seems to elude us. This discovery is worth all the wealth of the earth, for it is a treasure of heaven. In our endless search for something to fill the void in our hearts and heal our spirits, I am convinced we will one day discover the answer is simple—love. Without it, even the wealthiest of men have little.

Love is more than the foundation of achieving happiness; it is also the fundamental principle for achieving true wealth. If we lose ourselves in loving and serving others, our priorities and passions will settle into their proper places, almost as if by magic. In the words of R. Roy Keaton, "Too many people forget that the supreme duty of every man is to make a life, since almost anyone can make a living."[7]

Thus, the first amazing treasure heralds this truth from the catacombs of eternity:

In your quest for monetary satisfaction, in your coming and going, and in all your getting, never forget this one spiritual thing: life's greatest treasures lie hidden within your own heart and within the humble walls of your own home. Remember that love is more potent than force, it is more compelling than fierce and mighty armies, and it is finer than any earthly possessions. Therefore, resolve to love and love often. Begin to dispense the amazing treasure of love today, for with it no man will have a more joyous and rich tomorrow.

Notes

1. Ralph Waldo Emerson in *Richard Evans' Quote Book* (Salt Lake City: Publishers Press, 1971), 183.
2. Karl F. Kuhn and Theo Koupelis, *In Quest of the Universe* (Boston: Jones & Bartlett Publishers, 2004).
3. Victor Frankl, *Man's Search for Meaning* (New York: Simon & Schuster, 1984), 57, emphasis in original.
4. Henry Drummond in *Treasury of the World's Great Sermons*, comp.

Warren W. Wiersbe (Grand Rapids: Kregel Publications, 1977), 185–86.

5. Brigham Young, "Very Few Will Inherit Celestial Glory," *Journal of Discourses*, vol. 18 (accessed Jan. 8, 2009: http://journalofdiscourses.org/Vol_18/JD18-212.html)
6. Ezra Taft Benson, *Sermons and Writings of President Ezra Taft Benson* (Salt Lake City: Intellectual Reserve, 2003), 274–75.
7. R. Roy Keaton in *Richard Evans' Quote Book* (Salt Lake City: Publishers Press, 1971), 229.

"I am the better man, having been loved by a goodly woman. My courage is unequaled among the King's finest Knights, because she believes in me. She has freed my wings to soar unchallenged in my little world, because she has given herself to me." —*Jeffrey Dale Hair*

Amazing Treasure Number Two

Marriage: Your Mona Lisa Masterpiece

"Winning a love once is not enough. Keep *rewinning* it. . . . In the last analysis, it's up to you to save your marriage."[1]

Recently, a friend said to me, "Jeff, you will succeed in life because your wife loves and supports you. You're a team. She sends you out of the castle each morning as her prince, which gives you the power to conquer the dragons of the world. You are undivided, and as a result, together you will overcome the obstacles and challenges that lie before you."

He continued, "On the other hand I will fail at many things because my wife fails to see me in the same light. Regrettably, I am not her prince, but she's not exactly what I wanted either. My wife and I are divided and so we will not achieve the fulness of our potential."

It was my observation his wife was an affectionate and wonderful woman. So I said, "That's an excuse and you know it! What you and your wife need is a little love from each other. When was the last time you sent her flowers?"

"Oh no, I don't do flowers," he interrupted.

"Send your wife some flowers or I'll send them in your behalf," I said.

He conceded to send flowers. He stubbornly refused to give her roses, so he compromised and gave her three carnations. When he handed them to her, she was suspicious. But after reassuring her he had no ulterior motive, she relaxed and was her fun self again—in fact, he recounted she was more pleasant and affectionate than she had been for years. But he gave up too soon. Several days later, he came to work indignant, and firmly stated, "That's the last time I ever waste that kind of money. The flowers are dead, and she's back to her old ways already."

Instead of becoming a team with common purposes and goals, this husband and wife are disconnected and constantly pulling against each other. There is no energy or magic; there is no wind beneath wings, no soaring. Each has grounded the other. It is not surprising both parties feel unfulfilled and unhappy in their marriage. For compensation they turn to other sources to fill the void. In this divided and lonely state, they have become vulnerable to the tempting allure of materialism.

On another occasion, I watched an associate of mine, whom I will call Tom, pull into a parking plaza with his wife. He parked, stepped out of the vehicle, and began to walk across the parking plaza. His wife had to let herself out and try to catch up. Never once did Tom turn to acknowledge her, to look to see where she was, or slow down. When she walked by, the expression on her face revealed everything. She felt humiliated and degraded. It seemed as though Tom was ashamed of her, and she was painfully aware of it. She walked with eyes down. The sight tore at me. I wished I could have reached out to her and offered encouragement. I wanted to try to heal the nasty wounds that had been inflicted upon her—not by an enemy—by her own husband. John Ruskin once said, "Do not think you can make a girl lovely if you do not make her happy."[2]

I have often wondered how any man can justify breaking the heart and spirit of the precious woman who willing gave herself to him. Our companions should be the recipients of our finest efforts. Concerning this sacred duty, Abraham Lincoln once promised, "Whatever woman may cast her lot with mine, should any ever do so, it is my intention to do all in my power to make her happy and contented; and there is nothing I can imagine that would make me more unhappy than to fail in this effort."[3]

Some years ago I counseled with an impressive young man who had been struggling in a menial career and needed a sounding board. Stan was honorable and his work ethic was impeccable. He was naturally good with people and had a razor-sharp mind. I spent an evening convincing my friend of the unlimited potential and talent I saw in him. He could do anything if he applied himself. With the doors to his imagination open, he saw himself fulfilling his dream as a medical doctor. He could barely contain the excitement. Determined to pay the price, he rushed home to share the good news with his wife.

I saw Stan a few days later and asked about his wife's response. Embarrassed, he admitted she had laughed at him. She had said, "You Stan? Have you gone crazy? You need to pull your head out of the clouds and stop dreaming. No one knows you better than I do, and you don't have what it takes to be a doctor."

Stan was never the same after this discussion with his wife. In the presence of an encouraging friend, he believed he could conquer medical school. When his spouse finished with him, he resigned himself to the brainless job that he so hated. He effectively folded back his wings and quietly cowered into the coop with the rest of the chickens. "I have spread my dreams under your feet; tread softly because you tread on my dreams."[4]

Wives of Latter-day leaders have lovingly walked in the shadow of the Lord's anointed since the restoration. In every sense of the word they have served as intimate partners with the Lord in their husband's evolution. I'm personally acquainted with a story of one revered man's courting days with his wife. After the first date or so, the girl's grandfather pulled her aside and expressed his belief that she could do better than this seemingly average young man.

Was the observation of the grandfather wrong regarding his granddaughter's new suitor? Or is it possible that she looked beyond the boyish awkwardness and saw tremendous potential? History would prove that she partnered with the Lord in the transformation of this rather ordinary young man into a man of God.

I have a beautiful letter written by my "princess," my wife. It has been as inspiring to me as my patriarchal blessing:

> What do you think the miracle of love is? A question whispered as we danced, holding each other close in the dark. I have so many answers now, a different one for every year we've been together, and I know there are more.
>
> Back then love was a handsome gentleman with red hair, full of mystery and beautiful words. Love soon became an ambitious young man full of hope and eager to conquer life. Everything was new, full of wonder, yet also wrought with uncertainty and awkward beginnings. Love was a man full of insight and compassion who helped us both

> through these new beginnings.
>
> Before long, "our love" as we came to call it, started to grow. It was springtime, full of new life, adventure, color, flowers, showers, and a baby boy. Love was a man struggling and questioning, never giving up. A man who would learn to nurture, a man who would find answers to his questions and solutions for his problems, a man who would make things happen.
>
> Love matured, no longer new, but knowing and blooming, changing and growing. Sunshine and baby girls filled our world with ribbons of pink and soft whispers of changing seasons. Love is a man who is like the wind, restless and daring, always changing, stirring up all in its path, a man who would realize achievement of goals and dreams, and dream more dreams, climbing and racing and moving on.
>
> Love is sacrifice, love is acceptance, love is struggling, crying together, and sometimes crying alone. Love is holding on and letting go. Love is a man who can find a light in the darkest night and hold it up with an outstretched hand, beckoning, beseeching, and helping me find love in unlikely places. Love is a man with all the strength of a hurricane who can also be as soft and gentle as a caressing breeze.
>
> Twelve years later, love is a holey, tattered dish towel, noisy children with dirty clothes and tousled hair, a broken picture frame, a crowded home, a deflated balloon in a balloon bouquet, a dented television set, a partially working stereo, a love note on wrinkled paper, a less than perfect figure, no tractor, no piano, a less than perfect life, and a beautiful man who makes it all seem so much better than perfect.
>
> I look out at the stars and remember words that linger from a glorious day and a far away place . . . "out of all the stars in the heavens, worlds without end, people as numerous as the sands on the seashore, and you two found each other." I am only beginning to understand the miracle![5]

My friend was right about one thing: I will succeed in facing the challenges of life because I am blessed with the unconditional love of my wife. Pamela believes in me and I know it. As my friend stated, what dragon in life can stop me! I am loved beyond my capacity to receive. Her belief has transformed this frog into her prince.

Herein lies the great and hidden secret for affecting human behavior. I will literally wear myself out to become what she sees me as. She doesn't need to push or prod. I am motivated to do and be better because I don't want to disappoint her. My potential is largely defined by what she sees in me. As Joseph Smith said, "When persons manifest the least kindness and love to me, O what power it has over my mind, while the opposite course has a tendency to harrow up all the harsh feelings and depress the human mind."[6]

If you are to ever experience the wonderful magic of this powerful treasure, you must learn to love your partner unconditionally. If your marriage is to endure and blossom into something rare and beautiful, it will be up to the only person you have any control over—you! Thomas Carlyle said, "Over the time thou hast no power, . . . solely over one man therein thou hast a quite absolute, uncontrollable power; him redeem, him make honest."[7]

How many marriages end with one or both partners claiming they need time and freedom to "find themselves"? In reality what they're seeking is fulfillment and happiness—goals that elude the selfish. Instead, treat your companion the way you wish to be treated and only then will you find yourself. "For whosoever will save his life shall lose it: and whosoever will lose his life for my sake shall find it" (Matthew 16:25).

To those who are married I ask, which condition is the greatest investment of your eternal portfolio? Does your life's canvas portray bitter or broken hearts? Or have your expert brush strokes created a Mona Lisa masterpiece? Under heaven and earth you will not possess a more priceless asset. Despite life's hardships, is your spouse happier and better off since trustingly accepting your offer years ago? Instead of constantly nagging and dwelling on negatives, accentuate the positive and your partner will one day rise up and become exactly what you see in him.

On one occasion, I assisted a soft-spoken but brilliant friend to the airport. As we made our way, he asked me how my wife and family were doing. I answered my wife was an angel and I loved her more than words could express. He turned and with a degree of urgency said, "Jeff, does she know exactly how you feel?"

"Yes, sir," I replied.

"Have you told her recently," he asked, "because one day you could lose that special privilege? Tell her today, Jeff, and tell it to her often. She needs to hear it daily." I was aware his wife had died recently. I also knew they had cultivated something special and were very close. When together, which was often, they were always holding hands and smiling. I noticed a spark missing from his countenance after her death. Although life wasn't the same without his princess, he moved forward with great courage and faith.

I dropped him off at the terminal and agreed to pick him up in a few days. I said a little prayer for this lonely man and then promptly went about my day. The day for his return finally arrived, and that morning I awoke with a singular thought upon my mind: "When you see my husband today tell him I love him." Puzzled, I brushed it off and went about my day. That night I picked him up at the airport. In stark contrast to his optimistic mood en route to the airport, he was now subdued. In fact, he barely spoke a word. I felt certain he was missing his wife and recalled the thought I had that morning and wondered if I should convey it to him. "But this is a wise man," I reasoned. "Surely he will think I am presumptuous. Of course he knows his wife loves him!"

When we arrived at our destination he got out and thanked me politely. As he turned to walk away I attempted to tell him again, but failed. Ashamed, I wished him goodnight, jumped into the car, and started to drive away. Suddenly something overcame me. I abruptly applied the brakes, jumped out of the vehicle and ran back to him. "Pardon me," I blurted, "I, I awoke this morning with a strong impression that, that I needed to tell you your wife loves you very much. I know you must already know this, but I felt impressed to tell you my experience." A gentle smile swept across his face and a twinkle lit his eyes. He gave me a big hug and thanked me for not passing up such an opportunity. I believe he was missing her terribly. She knew it and found a way to reach around his pain and loneliness to touch her prince with the assurance of her love—expressed audibly by another human voice.

Invest in each other. Take the necessary time to build and encourage. Send flowers and notes of love and appreciation. It is the spontaneous execution of little acts of kindness that keeps two hearts actively in love.

Patterned after celestial harmony, the second amazing treasure reveals this timeless truth:

"The sum which two married people owe to one another defies calculation. It is an infinite debt, which can only be discharged through all eternity."[8] Of all earth's breathless splendors, nothing is so beautiful and invincible as a man and woman who love, serve, and care for each other. In this blissful state, children need to be taught little else, and life's spears and arrows will never be fatal. There is no challenge the two cannot conquer, and heaven and earth will be blessed.

Search the great libraries and universities, and you will not see this idea taught as a principle of wealth. Yet it is among the finest.

Notes

1. Hubert S. Howe in *Richard Evans' Quote Book* (Salt Lake City: Publishers Press, 1971).
2. John Ruskin in *Richard Evans' Quote Book* (Salt Lake City: Publishers Press, 1971).
3. Abraham Lincoln in *Mary Todd Lincoln: A Biography* (accessed Jan. 8, 2009: http://marriage.about.com/od/presidentialmarriages/a/abelincoln_3.htm), 87.
4. "William Butler Yeats quotes," http://thinkexist.com/quotation/but_i-being_poor-have_only_my_dreams-i_have/145319.html
5. Pam Hair to Jeffrey Dale Hair (in the author's possession).
6. "Chapter 37: Charity, the Pure Love of Christ," *Teachings of the Presidents of the Church: Joseph Smith* (2007), 423–34.
7. Thomas Carlyle, "Self-control quotes," http://www.giga-usa.com/quotes/topics/self-control_t001.htm
8. "Johann Wolfgang von Goethe," http://en.wikiquote.org/wiki/Johann_Wolfgang_von_Goethe

"But seek ye first the kingdom of God, and his righteousness; and all these things shall be added unto you." Matthew 6:33

Amazing Treasure Number Three

Tithes & Offerings: Blessings from the Windows of Heaven

During His ministry, Jesus taught a powerful principle of finance.

> And they sent out unto him their disciples with the Herodians, saying, Master, we know that thou art true, and teachest the way of God in truth, neither carest thou for any man: for thou regardest not the person of men. Tell us therefore, What thinkest thou? Is it lawful to give tribute unto Caesar, or not? But Jesus perceived their wickedness, and said, Why tempt ye me, ye hypocrites? Shew me the tribute money. And they brought unto him a penny. And he saith unto them, Whose is the image and superscription? They say unto him, Caesar's. Then saith he unto them, Render therefore unto Caesar the things which are Caesar's; and unto God the things that are God's. When they had heard these words, they marveled, and left him, and went their way. (Matthew 22:16–22)

"Thou shalt truly tithe all the increase of the seed, that the field bringeth forth year by year" (Deuteronomy 14:22).

The Church has become one of the most financially sound institutions in the world. But it was not always this way. President Lorenzo Snow was faced with a growing membership, mounting debt, and a drought that affected much of central and southern Utah. Many Church members in these areas were near ruin. President Snow turned to the Lord for guidance. After much prayer and fasting, the Lord's answer came in a strange way: The burdened Saints would be given an additional financial obligation—tithing.

Thereafter, President Snow traveled about the depressed regions, preaching the divine principle of paying an honest tithe—returning to God that which is God's. Tithing always has been an act of faith. President Snow was faced with instructing people that were near starvation to pay a full tenth of their meager income or poor harvests to the Lord. The prophet's counsel defied conventional wisdom. Nevertheless, the Lord's ways are not the ways of man. God will test the faith of His people through trial and hardship. There will be times when He will require us to leave the well-lit arena of worldly wisdom and safety and walk into the darkness where faith is tried and perfected and promised blessings are received.

As the people obeyed the prophet, the drought abated and the Church was eventually released from financial bondage. Through the principle of tithing, the Church has become a solid financial institution, building chapels and temples that cover the world. The Lord states, "Will a man rob God? Yet ye have robbed me. But ye say, Wherein have we robbed thee? In tithes and offerings. Ye are cursed with a curse: for ye have robbed me, even this whole nation" (Malachi 3:8–9).

Another of the many blessings associated with the law of tithing was taught by Joseph F Smith. "One of the best ways that I know of to pay my obligations to my brother, my neighbor, or business associate, is for me first to pay my obligations to the Lord. . . . If you desire to prosper, and to be free men and women and a free people, first meet your just obligations to God, and then meet your obligations to your fellowmen."[1]

Like the Saints in drought-stricken southern Utah, we too must first obey the law of tithing to receive a testimony of its power and truthfulness. "Jesus answered them, and said, my doctrine is not mine, but he that sent me. If any man will do his will he shall know of the doctrine, whether it be of God, or whether I speak of myself" (John 7: 16–17).

Concerning tithes and offerings, the Lord promises that the windows of heaven will open and that He will pour out blessings so great that we will not have room to contain them. That is a powerful promise! Gordon B. Hinckley added this counsel,

> The Lord will open the windows of heaven according to our need, and not according to our greed. If we are paying tithing to get rich, we

> are doing it for the wrong reason. The basic purpose for tithing is to provide the Church with the means needed to carry on His work. The blessing to the giver is an ancillary return and that blessing may not be always in the form of financial or material benefit. There are many ways in which the Lord can bless us beyond the riches of the world.

The law of tithing was never intended to compensate us for personal financial failure or recklessness. Moreover, it is irresponsible to expect that the Lord will give us what we want or all we see our neighbors possess because we pay an honest tithe. Such a mentality will surely lead us into debt, turmoil, and even bitterness. Unless we are carefully guarding against it, greed can corrupt this divine principle. God will bless us, of this we can rest assured, but it will be on His terms and not ours—according to our need and not greed.

One distinguished leader of my acquaintance kept a genuine widow's mite on his desk to remind him of the sacred nature of tithes. I believe it motivated him to find and eliminate waste and to use tithing funds in a sacred manner.

Years ago I gave a homeless man temporary shelter in a shed located on my little farm. It was warm, dry, and had some modern conveniences. Previously he had been sleeping in shrubs surrounding businesses and chapels. Upon learning of the new unorthodox neighbor, a few locals were known to give Uncle Dewey a bad time as he pushed his bike around town. On one particularly bad day, he returned to my place in tears and said he better leave before he got me into more trouble with the neighbors. I talked him into staying until he got his feet under him a little better. One snowy night, close to Christmas, I received a knock at the door and found a scout leader and his troop standing on my front porch. Because Uncle Dewey had already retired for the night, they left the several boxes of food and clothing they brought for him in my care. As they were leaving, I asked them what ward they were affiliated with. They smiled and said they were with a protestant church on the other side of town and expressed uncertainty as to the meaning of the word "ward." As I stood there in the night looking at Uncle Dewey's lonely shed, I thanked God for inspired leaders. "Those boys are in good hands," I thought. They had gathered offerings from friends and fellow church members and distributed them to the truly needy.

> Then shall the King say unto them on his right hand, Come, ye blessed of my Father, inherit the kingdom prepared for you from the

> foundation of the world: For I was an hungred, and ye gave me meat: I was thirsty, and ye gave me drink: I was a stranger, and ye took me in: Naked, and ye clothed me: I was sick, and ye visited me: I was in prison, and ye came unto me. Then shall the righteous answer him, saying, Lord, when saw we thee an hungred, and fed thee? Or thirsty, and gave thee drink? When saw we thee a stranger, and took thee in? or naked, and clothed thee? Or when saw we thee sick, or in prison, and came unto thee? And the King shall answer and say unto them, Verily I say unto you, Inasmuch as ye have done it unto one of the least of these my brethren, ye have done it unto me. (Matthew 25:34–40)

Giving a generous fast offering is only one way of participating in this edict from the Lord. Paying tithes and offerings helps us maintain balance in our lives. It provides us an opportunity to show the Lord that we love Him more than our material substance. "As for me and my house," I want the Lord on my side; I want Him to pour out blessings from the windows of heaven upon me and my family. Furthermore, I don't believe in robbing Him or neglecting His poor. In the eternal scope of things, how can this be a prudent strategy?

As the saints in southern Utah faithfully followed the prophet, they discovered the miraculous and certain promise of the third amazing treasure:

"Bring ye all the tithes into the storehouse, that there may be meat in my house: and prove me now herewith, saith the Lord of hosts, if I will not open you the windows of heaven, and pour you out blessings, that there shall not be room enough to receive it. And I will rebuke the devourer for your sakes, and he shall not destroy the fruits of your ground; neither shall your vine cast her fruit before the time in the field, saith the Lord of Hosts" (Malachi 3:10–11). Tithing and offerings are eternal principles and when we align ourselves with them, specific blessings are bestowed upon us.

Who can doubt the divinity and power of this treasure? Surely not those who have exercised faith, opened their hearts, and tested the Lord by paying an honest tithe and offering.

Notes

1. "Chapter 19," *Teachings of the Presidents of the Church: Joseph F. Smith* (1998), 166.
2. Gordon B. Hinckley, "Tithing: An Opportunity to Prove Our Faithfulness," *Ensign*, May 1982.

"And I will say to my soul, soul, thou hast much goods laid up for many years; take thine ease, eat, drink, and be merry. But God said unto him, thou fool, this night thy soul shall be required of thee; then whose shall those things be." Luke 12:19–20

Amazing Treasure Number Four

Debt: To Be Rich Is to Owe Nothing!

"If there is any one thing that will bring peace and contentment into the human heart, and into the family, it is to live within our means,"[1] Heber J. Grant said. For a rapidly growing sector of Americans, the "American dream" has become increasingly elusive. Widespread availability to easy credit has given us enough rope to collectively hang ourselves. Even as I speak, record numbers of people are dangling from debt's insidious gallows while countless others temporarily skirt the noose of the unforgiving henchman. Instead of reversing our predicament by applying time-honored principles, many prolong and worsen their misery by engaging in the art of so-called "creative financing." Rather than cutting back, they apply for more plastic and loans and dig the hole deeper and deeper.

Over the past several years, we have robbed the equity from our homes and with smoke and mirrors mortgaged our future for luxuries that we could and should have gone without. Soon, even dependable Peter has nothing for us to rob to pay the ever-nagging Paul. Too many of us are months or weeks away from ruin. Few of us have resisted partaking of easy credit.

Remember the childhood story of the songbird that traded feathers for worms to an entrepreneurial cat? The cat claimed that his solitary desire was to help little birdies in need. "You deserve easier worms" was his never-ending slogan. After several weeks the songbird had foolishly traded so many feathers and become so plump she could no longer fly. One day when the sly cat was hungry, he ate the crippled songbird.

Like the songbird, how many of us have awakened to find heartless creditors with hunger in their eyes, and we, because of the weight of debt chained around our necks, are unable to take flight? Poor decisions have turned our dreams into nightmares. Henrik Ibsen said, "There can be no freedom or beauty about a home life that depends on borrowing and debt."[2]

When our goal in life has narrowed to chasing wealth, it can make us greedy, rob us of peace, or, in extreme cases, send us to prison or the soup line. As an alternative, the amazing treasures in this book will significantly improve the life and happiness of the average working individual and family.

Today, debt has become public enemy number one. To combat it, I will now reveal my top-secret, highly effective formula that has taken me years of research to compile and perfect. It is one simple, yet powerful word—No! This word has incredible power. Say it to yourself: No. Say it often: no, no, no! Say no to loan institutions; say no to borrowing to upgrade your home or buy a better car; say no to borrowing for an exotic trip; say no to borrowing for the boat of your dreams; say no to eating out and charging the meal to your credit card; say no to borrowing for that big screen TV; say no to spending money on cable service; say no to a cell phone; say no to credit cards; say no to a new computer; say no to a motor home. Especially, be willing to say no to your children; say no, no, no to your ego. Can you feel this formula's potent power of delivery? Say no, and say it often!

It is worth repeating again and again; we must learn to value freedom and peace of mind paramount to having things. By saying no to yourself and others, you can begin to reclaim your life and one fine day truly call it your own. If you are tenacious and effective you will in time be indebted to no one. In this wonderful position of strength, everything will seem sweeter and more beautiful. Freedom must become your overriding desire and you must want it so badly that unnecessary material things no longer tempt you. Say no and take control of your life. The Lord of the universe has so eloquently spoken, "Pay the debt thou hast contracted. . . . Release thyself from bondage" (D&C 19:35).

Opponents to this idea are quick to say certain types of debt are good.

They assert consumer spending drives the U.S. economy and well-planned debt, like a mortgage, is okay. They say that we take on debt because we are confident in the future and in our capacity to pay it off. It's the American way! But as John Cunniff points out, we have foolishly moved beyond debt confidence and we now tread in the muddy realm of imprudence: "Credit card debts are high because people cannot get by without using the credit offered on their cards. And if they have to borrow now, what great event in the future, what windfall, will endow them with the money to pay off those debts? In short, will that old-fashioned confidence get people through all this? Will consumer confidence somehow be converted into a medium for buying things or paying bills?"[3]

Nearly a startling 144 million Americans collectively charged a whopping 1.5 trillion dollars in the year 2003 alone. The average American family owns eight credit cards and carries an average balance over $8,000. Fifty million cardholders pay off their debts completely at the end of each month. Loaning institutions refer to these highly responsible cardholders as "deadbeats." However, 90 million cardholders pay only a portion of their balances, and 35 million pay only the minimum payments. These desirable cardholders are referred to as "revolvers." This group is most profitable for credit card companies. Lending institutions spend a great deal of money tracking individual consumer habits to determine whether or not you're a "deadbeat" or a "revolver."

Have you ever closely examined your credit card contract? If so, did you understand anything you read? Unless you're a specialized lawyer, it was probably undecipherable. Many critics claim this is a tactic to intentionally keep consumers ignorant. The following are a few hidden points most generally contained in the fine print of credit card agreements: Issuer can raise interest rates after fifteen days' notice if you fail to make a payment to them or any other creditor, for example: mortgage, auto loans, or monthly services. One missed or late payment can trigger what is called a "Universal Default." This simply means the cardholder could be penalized by other creditors even though the default had nothing directly to do with him.

A loaning institution can raise interest rates on your credit card balances if the balances with third party institutions become too high. Under such penalties, interest rates can double or triple, reaching as high as 30 to 40 percent. With exorbitant interest accruing on all your accounts, the bludgeoning can continue with late fees, over-the-limit fees, and return check fees, often at 30 to 40 dollars per infraction. It is easy to see how a rather average family experiencing a financial setback, like a job loss, medical problem, or a family death or breakup, can trigger a domino effect that often ends in bankruptcy.

Utah has at times lead the nation in bankruptcies. Statistics reveal Utah's 2008 foreclosure filings were up 93 percent over those in 2007, substantially higher than the national average of 57 percent. This reckless trend cannot continue without causing serious repercussions for the future.

One of the greatest lies perpetrated is that life owes us something! We are told we are owed a better life and we can borrow our way into it. The money is not ours, but we deserve it as a depraved sort of American entitlement. We are allured by exciting commercials of fast cars, airline trips, and motor homes. New boats appear equipped with pretty girls and handsome men ready to party. Advertisers know how to spin this alluring web. Foolishly we get trapped in it, and so do our children. Marvin J. Ashton said, "We live in a self-indulgent, me-oriented, materialistic society. Advertisements entice young buyers by demonstrating how easy it is to get credit and buy on time. Interestingly, no ads focus on the glamour of paying the money back, nor do they mention how long or hard it is to do just that—especially with the unavoidable interest added on."[4]

To attempt this unattainable lifestyle, we use the equity in our homes, put our wives to work unnecessarily, and run up credit card balances. And we stretch ourselves further by taking possession of items now and putting off paying for them until months later. The creditor is come to take unto him my two sons (2 Kings 4:1).

Gordon B. Hinckley has also cautioned, "I have seen in a very vivid way the terrible tragedies of many who have gone on a binge of borrowing for things they really do not need. How many people might have been saved pain and misery, suffering, embarrassment, and trouble had they listened to counsel concerning personal debt."[5]

"Money, money, money, please come and spend my money," pipes the piper. Many foolishly partake of the forbidden poison. Sadly, it isn't until the victims are wrapped in a web of debt so tight that the piper shows his true character. He morphs into a harsh and unforgiving taskmaster, enslaving his victims and forcing them to pay back every single penny—with heavy interest.

> Interest never sleeps nor sickens nor dies; it never goes to the

> hospital; it works on Sundays and holidays; it never takes a vacation; it never visits nor travels; it takes no pleasure; it is never laid off work nor discharged from employment; it never works on reduced hours; it never has short crops nor droughts; it never pays taxes; it buys not food; it wears no clothes; it is un-housed and without home and so has no repairs, no replacements, no shingling, plumbing, painting, or white-washing; it has neither wife, mother, nor kinfolk to watch over and care for; it has no expense of living; it has neither weddings nor births nor deaths; it has no love, no sympathy; it is as hard and soulless as a granite cliff. Once in debt, interest is your companion every minute of the day and night; you cannot shun it or slip away from it; you cannot dismiss it; it yields neither to entreaties, demands, or orders; and whenever you get in its way or cross its course or fail to meet its demands, it crushes you.[6]

If unfortunate victims cannot meet their deadlines, the piper will torment them and rob them of peace. The piper will repossess their cars, homes, and anything of value, and put them out on the street. He will destroy their name and credit. It has been aptly said, "Poverty is hard but debt is horrible."

True to family tradition I took my family to the state fair one year. We saw small homemade items made by folks in little towns across the state. Farm animals, tractors, vegetables, and fruits were on display. The state fair is a celebration of the harvest and it provides a rare opportunity for city and country people to see how the other lives.

In the opening ceremonies, the governor gave a brief speech on what he believed was good and right about the fair and old-fashioned values. He reminisced about his years on the family farm and the valuable lessons he learned there. On one particular occasion, he asked his grandpa why the family couldn't expand the farm and purchase new equipment and machinery like so many of the other farmers in the region. His wise grandfather motioned his arm across the farmland and promised if the family would continue to pay as they went, they would still be farming long after debt-ridden farmers began to struggle or went belly up. The governor said time proved his grandfather right. As a result of his grandfather's thrift and foresight, the family was able to weather the many droughts and economic hardships the future brought. The governor's story is a valuable lesson for family economics. Do we pay as we go? Or do we stretch ourselves beyond wisdom? "Till thou hast paid the very last mite" (Luke 12:59).

Modern prophets have have pledged to keep the Church solvent and far, far away from debt. What a profound lesson we can all learn from observing these wise leaders. They pay as they go; they don't build temples or chapels faster than they have resources! The Church is a house of discipline and order; budgeting and restraint prevail. Howard W. Hunter also taught,

> The Church avoids debt. We don't rely on taxation to take care of our people. We believe that we should take care of our own and not rely upon the help of others. These newspaper reporters were interested in how we build without having any debt. We have built thousands of buildings in the world, and everyone is paid for in full. We have no indebtedness. The Church has always taught us that we should live within our income and be fee from debt, and it practices what it preaches.[7]

Parents have been counseled by the Lord to have a house of order and to prepare for every needful thing (D&C 88:119).

If you are still unconvinced of debt's ability to cut your financial throat and make of your life a living hell, you may now lose future employment opportunities. Thirty-eight percent of employers check potential employees' credit ratings. Supporters of this practice say few things reveal the character of an individual more than how they control and manage their personal finances.

I was traveling through a rather affluent area with an elderly, successful attorney several years ago. Extravagant homes, toys, and luxury automobiles lined the streets. After several minutes of silence passed, he finally spoke, "How can these people afford to live this way? I fear many of them are deep in debt." He continued, "One of the happiest achievements of my life was the day my wife and I paid off the mortgage to our home. I would recommend it to anyone." "Owe no man anything" (Romans 13:8).

Again, some of us unwittingly refer to a mortgage as good debt. I concede that debt for a home is sometimes necessary for a time, but the hair on the back of my neck rises when debt is called *good*. Reason dictates that beyond a few extraordinary purchases like a home we should pay as we go. Wisdom dictates we should pay off these debts as soon as possible. "I may venture to suggest that you do not speculate. Let every head of every household aim to own his own home, free from mortgage."[8]

> What a wonderful feeling it is to be free of debt, to have a little

> money put away where it can be retrieved when necessary for an emergency. I think of a number of astute individuals who have followed such a practice personally. One man told me about a mortgage he had on his home that was drawing 4 percent interest. Financial consultants told him it was foolish to pay off that mortgage when it carried so low a rate of interest. But the first opportunity he had to acquire some means, he and his wife determined they would pay off the mortgage. He has been free of debt since that day—which I believe has contributed, over time, to his subsequent financial comfort and, more importantly, to a sense of great personal freedom and peace of mind. I believe it is one reason that he wears a smile on his face and whistles while he works.[9]

It is worth highlighting that the man in this particular example did not speculate with his money until after his home was paid in full. Robert G. Ingersoll gave us this insight: "A mortgage casts a shadow on the sunniest field."[10]

Personal sacrifice brings forth blessings. Tucked somewhere inside a filing cabinet in our home is an amortization chart for our old, retired mortgage. The several pages are well worn. Dozens of colorful lines appear on each page signifying payment in full for the corresponding months. Today it has the appearance of an old war map. I vividly remember paying the mortgage company ten dollars to print and send it to me; it proved to be one of the best investments we ever made. With this chart we were able to clearly see how much interest we were paying each month and the money we could save by doubling, tripling, or quadrupling the payments.

Many times my wife and I parted with what little extra money we had saved for the month and sent it in with the mortgage payment. Sometimes we barely made the regular payment, but we sacrificed whenever we could and eventually paid it off. To this day, my wife and I still get misty-eyed when we discuss days of being united toward achieving a difficult goal. Can you see yourself owning your home free and clear? We stayed focused month by month, year after year, until one day we were able to send off the final payment. Instead of thirty years, we paid off our mortgage in six. Rather than paying a couple hundred thousand dollars in interest, we paid only several thousand. The day we paid off the mortgage was one of the happiest days of our lives. Like the wise attorney, we too can recommend this to anyone. Thomas Fowell Buxton said, "I hold a doctrine, to which I owe not much, indeed, but all the little I ever had, namely, that with ordinary talent and extraordinary perseverance, all things are attainable."[11]

I offer a flashing red light warning: on your vigilant quest for freedom, absolutely do not purchase more house than is practical and comfortable for your needs, even if you qualify for it. Perhaps more than any decision you make in your life, this will have the most profound effect on your future financial stability.

Generally, lending limits are set at 28/36 percent. This simply means that your monthly mortgage payment cannot exceed 28 percent of your income, and your mortgage payment plus your other debts cannot exceed 36 percent of your income. I believe these numbers are too liberal and tend to make you house rich and cash poor. I personally prefer the old formula: 22/28. With a little commitment and foresight, a couple can lower this ratio to an even safer level. Never lose sight of the fact that these limits exist to protect you from taking on too much debt. Owning a home isn't as simple as making the mortgage payments. With ownership comes utilities, taxes, insurance, repairs, and furnishings, improvements, decorating, and making room for a growing family.

Keep in mind that borrowers and lenders do not figure into these formulas the payment of tithing, increasing taxes, and savings. How will this be possible if you push the envelope on the size of your mortgage? When borrowing for a mortgage, stay well within your income, even if you have to save longer for a larger down payment.

For several years many people thought I was poorer than a church mouse because I lived in a small, older house and drove a beat-up, old vehicle. Success was not apparent because I was in the preparatory stage of my financial life. Even so I didn't let other people's opinions change my well-planned strategy. I continued to march to the beat of my own drummer. When you are in the process of finding a home, look for something practical. You might need to swallow a little pride, but why should you care? You have a clear strategy that will lead you to freedom and happiness.

Before looking for a home, make a list of priorities and simple things that are important. Put more emphasis on the spirit or feeling of the home rather than its size or prestigious appearance. Remember, much of your future happiness depends upon getting this decision correct.

If a castle makes people happy, then why are many so sad? I know a couple who destroyed their financial future because of poor decisions.

During their engagement, Jenny and Harry (names have been changed) looked for a house to call home. After they returned from a house-shopping date one night, Harry quietly pulled me aside and expressed concern about Jenny's expensive taste in homes. He had hoped to begin married life in a modest house and work his way up to a dream home. But Jenny was adamantly opposed. She wanted her dream house now!

A few years into their marriage, Jenny eventually got her way. They borrowed everything they could from various institutions, and borrowed more from relatives. They erected a mansion in the middle of a humble farming community where Harry had been transferred. The locals were angry at such an ostentatious display in the middle of the humble community. After a couple of stressful years, Harry and Jenny realized they could no longer afford the house. Unable to make the monthly payments, they were forced to put the house up for sale. But the castle was the largest home in the community and was impossible to sell. They ended up selling it for much less than they owed. Unfortunately, for the rest of their lives they will be paying back institutions and family for a home they no longer own. Despite the fact they are good people, attend church, and pay tithing, it must be remembered man is seldom, if ever, separated from the consequences of his actions.

Another family heeded the wise counsel to get out of debt. They sold their expensive home located in an exclusive neighborhood and used the equity to purchase outright a modest home in a different part of town. No more mortgage payments! The action of this couple took faith and courage, but they were more concerned about obeying a prophet than impressing neighbors. They have come to realize that happiness comes from obeying the Lord by following His prophet.

After years of sacrifice, my wife and I had been looking for a larger home in a rather affluent area. I took a wise old friend named Neil Knight, to look over the physical soundness of the house and in the end he gave me his overall impression. "Jeff," he said, "it's a beautiful home, but you can't afford to live here." Proudly, I pointed out the substantial down payment we had saved and how it would bring the mortgage payment down to a manageable amount. But he only repeated himself, "Jeff, you still can't afford to live here."

He explained the kids in this neighborhood lived a life of luxury, and he asked me if I could afford to duplicate it considering my current income level. He said, "These families travel all over the world on vacations. Their kids receive new and expensive cars for birthdays and graduations. These children will be your children's friends. Will you try to give your children the same kinds of things?" Even though my wife and I had sacrificed many years to provide our children with a beautiful home in an exclusive area, my friend explained that they would not understand or appreciate any of it. Instead, they would feel deprived if we couldn't give them the lifestyle their new friends would enjoy. "You may be able to afford to peek into the world of the people in this neighborhood, but in the end you will be doing your children a great disservice," he said. On the other hand, he explained that if we were to choose a more modest neighborhood, my children would feel blessed, happy, and comfortable.

I am so grateful for the insight and courage of my good friend Neil for saying what needed to be said. I have no question now that he prevented me from making one of the biggest mistakes of my life. Thank you, Neil Knight! I have tried to broadcast your wisdom to all who would open their hearts and listen.

Debt, let my people go! Historically, God's people have either been destroyed or led into bondage when they failed to obey His prophets. Is not debt a form of enslavement? Our forefathers valued freedom above life itself. "I have sworn upon the altar of God eternal hostility against every form of tyranny over the mind of man," said Thomas Jefferson.[12] Debt is a form of tyranny over the mind of man and purchase by purchase, many of us march toward its prison.

Are we listening or are we foolishly stepping into captivity? If so, we must stop, rally our resources, pray fervently, and come out fighting to regain our freedom. It is written, "No man can serve two masters; for either he will hate the one and love the other, or else he will hold to the one and despise the other. Ye cannot serve God and Mammon" (3 Nephi 13:24).

One day during my two-year mission, my companion and I were busy setting up teaching appointments for a training exchange we were planning with another set of elders, when we happened upon a beautiful home in the countryside. We knocked on the front door and were invited in to meet the owner. He was charming. On display throughout his house were expensive treasures from distant places. Everything was extraordinarily beautiful. He was learned. He seemed noble. After inviting him to hear our message, he explained he had prior arrangements but agreed to meet with us the following evening. After parting, we spoke of how wonderful it would be if this gentleman joined the Church.

As we traveled down the winding country road on our way home, an old abandoned house, that I hadn't noticed before, caught my attention. The surrounding grounds were overgrown with tall weeds, and old rusty junk was strewn about the yard. As we passed by, I remember thinking what a contrast this house was to the estate of the rich man.

We exchanged companions with the other set of missionaries as planned. My new companion and I arrived for the much-anticipated appointment. We approached the doors, knocked, and waited with anticipation. Nobody answered. I knocked again, this time longer and louder. Still nothing! It appeared as if nobody was home. We walked around the yard hoping to find someone, but to no avail. The thought had never crossed my mind that the man would not keep his appointment. Without a backup plan, we got back into the car and started to drive—where I did not know.

Soon, we passed the old, rundown house. Something urged me to stop. "What a ridiculous notion," I thought. The prompting persisted, "Go back." Again I ignored it. Nobody could possibly live there, I reasoned. To be completely forthright, I didn't want to appear uninspired or desperate in the eyes of the inexperienced missionary who was my companion for the night. But, when the thought came a third time, I grudgingly applied the brakes and turned around.

"What are you doing?" asked my companion.

"Following a crazy feeling," I replied, too embarrassed to say more. We knocked on the old, weathered door and waited. Nothing happened. I knocked again and again. Feeling confused and humiliated, I turned to leave, then hearing a faint sound inside, we stopped and waited. The door slowly opened. A bent-over, aged woman in a well-worn dress stood framed in the doorway. We introduced ourselves as LDS missionaries, and she immediately invited us in.

The front room was small, dark, and stale. The wooden floors creaked under our weight as we moved to a worn, dusty couch. She motioned for us to have a seat, and we reluctantly followed her lead.

"What on earth am I doing here? In her current state, this old, feeble woman is not much good to anyone, and besides, she can hardly hear," I reasoned to myself.

Pulling out my flip chart, I decided to give a quick lesson and leave. However, something was wrong. Although I had given the lesson many times, for some reason the words eluded me. In silence, we sat as beads of sweat ran down my forehead. Again, I dug deep, but nothing came. Offering a silent prayer, I stepped away from pride and gave my mind over to the Spirit. Suddenly, thoughts began to formulate. Looking into the eyes of the little old woman, I said with authority, "We are personal representatives of the Lord Jesus Christ. We are His servants and on His errand. He has sent us here and wants you to know of His love. He has not forgotten you. He is mindful of your sadness and loneliness."

With these simple words, the woman put her head down and wept. When she regained her composure, she recounted the tragic events of her life, including the untimely death of her husband. The last of her living relatives had just been killed in an auto accident, leaving her alone, and the weight was more than she could bear. She continued, "The other night I was feeling abandoned, sad, and lonely; so I knelt down and prayed that the Lord would comfort me. I know I shouldn't have bothered Him but the burden was more than I could manage."

My companion and I were now sitting up straight and listening intently to every word. "Later that night," she continued, "I had a dream that the Lord would send two young men in bright white shirts with a message for me." She wept again, but this time she was not alone. "For as the heavens are higher than the earth, so are my ways higher than your ways, and my thoughts than your thoughts" (Isaiah 55:9).

Few times in my life have I been as awestruck as I was in that little shack nestled in the Smokey Mountains. I felt the Lord near. What a profound lesson for two twenty-year-old boys! The rich man with his mansion and sprawling estate did not bother to receive the young messengers of the Lord. But the lonely, feeble woman in the rickety old shack, without worldly wealth, received the attention of heaven and the compassion of the Lord in response to her humble prayer.

As I pondered on this over the next few days, I came to realize that the Lord looks inward to the heart of man and not at the thickness of his wallet. Outwardly, the rich man owned much and the world respected and paid homage to him. But God's considerations are not those of the world. "And he looked up, and saw the rich men casting their gifts into the treasury. And he saw also a certain poor widow casting in thither two mites. And he said, Of a truth I say unto you, that this poor widow hath cast in more than they all: For all these have of their abundance cast in unto the offerings of God: but she of her penury hath cast in all the living that she had" (Luke 21:1–4).

Conversely, He states it is difficult for a rich man to enter into the kingdom of God. The pride which commonly accompanies wealth runs counter to divine attributes. On this monumental occasion, I was taught that the Lord is not impressed, as I was impressed, with worldly accomplishment or wealth. He is concerned with the quality of the soul. Jesus counseled one wealthy man, who had done much good, to give away all he had to the poor and come and follow him. But, for pride, ego, or whatever reason, the wealthy man could not do it. Perhaps we would do well to remember that Jesus, the Creator and Savior of the world, did not own a large, fancy home or any home for that matter. "And Jesus said unto him, The foxes have holes, and birds of the air have nests; but the Son of man hath not where to lay his head" (Matthew 8:20).

The only offering the Lord requires is inward—a broken heart and a contrite spirit. One memorable day in my life, He sent two of his personal representatives to a poor, old woman who needed His help. It became apparent to me He loved her unconditionally. Why should we expect anything different?

In the eternal scheme of things, wouldn't you forego the riches and hollow praise of this world to one day have a personal delegation of the Lord personally witness to you that He loves and hasn't left you alone? I would live in a humble shack or do whatever is required to win this most prized treasure. I can't think of anything more thrilling than to receive such a heavenly assurance and manifestation.

As the North Star is to the seafarer, there is no financial advice more accurate and reliable to the seeker than the fourth amazing treasure. It states:

"I have discovered the philosopher's stone that turns everything into gold: it is—pay as you go."[13] *Therefore, let us return to the dreamy view that our houses are cozy little cottages where love abounds, where we raise our children happily, where we plant gardens, and hang memories on the walls, and grow old together. Let us move away from the bankrupt mentality that we are what we own or that our living structures are monuments to ourselves, grand extensions of our egos.*

May God bless us to have the necessary wisdom and strength to take firm control of our lives, do what needs to be done, and one fine day live free from financial enslavement.

Notes

1. Heber J. Grant, "Mormon Economics," *The Improvement Era* (Salt Lake City: The Deseret News Press, 1969), 111.
2. Henrik Ibsen in *Richard Evans' Quote Book* (Salt Lake City: Publishers Press, 1971), 228.
3. John Cunniff, "Charting confidence of Americans deep in debt," *The Journal Record* (Oklahoma City, Mar. 25, 1997).
4. Marvin J. Ashton "One for the Money: Guide to Family Finance" (Salt Lake City: Intellectual Reserve, 1992).
5. Gordon B. Hinckley, "This I Believe" (Speech at Brigham Young University, Mar. 1, 1992).
6. J. Reuben Clark Jr, in Conference Report, Apr. 1938, 103.
7. Howard W. Hunter, "Economics and Welfare Principles," *The Teachings of Howard W. Hunter* (Salt Lake City: Bookcraft, 2002), 157.
8. J. Reuben Clark Jr, Jan. 1938.
9. Gordon B. Hinckley, *Standing for Something* (New York: Random House, 2000), 87.
10. Robert G. Ingersoll in *Richard Evans' Quote Book* (Salt Lake City: Publishers Press, 1971), 228.
11. Sir Thomas Fowell Buxton, "Perseverance quotes" http://www.giga-usa.com/quotes/topics/perseverance_t001.htm.
12. "Thomas Jefferson on Christianity & Religion," comp. Jim Walker, http://nobeliefs.com//jefferson.htm.
13. John Randolph, "Global Financial Advisor," http://www.globalfinancial-advisory.com/news.html.

"Sometimes when I consider what tremendous consequences come from little things–I am tempted to think there are no little things."
—Bruce Barton[1]

Amazing Treasure Number Five

Pennies: The Explosive Power of Small Things

Bud Walton, of the famed Walmart department stores, once said about his brother Sam (one of the wealthiest men ever to live): "People can't understand why we're still so conservative. They make a big deal about Sam being a billionaire and driving an old pickup truck or buying his clothes at Walmart or refusing to fly first class. It's just the way we were brought up. When a penny is lying out there on the street, how many people go out and pick it up? I'll bet I would. And I know Sam would."[2]

A billionaire picking up copper Lincolns? Sam Walton certainly did not need to bend down and pick up a stray penny. Apparently this self-made billionaire knows something that we should know and probably mimic. When was the last time you picked up a little copper penny? The answer to this question may determine whether or not you have the billionaire's wealth mentality.

Because he was poor, Sam wasn't handed the money to start his retail venture. He had to effectively squeeze water from rocks. He understood it took money to make money. Saving every penny he could to launch his venture, and then tending it carefully embedded within him the value of pennies. Getting into the habit of placing value on small things helped Sam Walton transform a small five-and-dime store into a mammoth retail chain. Brigham Young obviously understood this principle when he said, "Pick up everything, let nothing go to waste."[3]

Alma not only understood the tremendous power of this treasure but he understood that many people would consider the concept foolishness when it was eventually presented to them: "Now ye may suppose that this is foolishness in me; but behold I say unto you, that by small and simple things are great things brought to pass; and small means in many instances doth confound the wise" (Alma 37:6).

While serving my mission in Asheville, North Carolina, I came to know a rather wealthy and distinguished individual named Oliver Davis. Although Brother Davis was a man of substantial holdings, no one would know to meet him. It was common to see him walking down the street or driving his twenty-year-old Ford Falcon. Yet he was a man of considerable understanding, vision, and means. Rather than owning nice cars and toys, Brother Davis devoted countless hours and personal wealth to the Church's missionary effort. During a correlation meeting with local priesthood leaders one Sunday, a rather substantial check passed in front of me. I couldn't help noticing it was written to the general missionary fund of the Church, and the generous donor was Oliver Davis. As I passed the check toward the presiding leader, a brother I was sitting near informed me his donations occurred on a regular basis. Brother Davis even purchased an expensive movie projector so my companion and I could play the *First Vision* and *Man's Search for Happiness* for investigators. Food, copies of the Book of Mormon, and boxes full of needed pamphlets magically appeared at our door. We had to be careful what we said around Brother Davis because he often read in between the lines and bought us things we really hadn't requested.

One morning, Brother Davis took my companion and me to a local restaurant for breakfast. As we approached the entrance, he spotted a penny on the pavement, bent down, and picked it up. I attempted to hide my humiliation. I thought, "We're in suits and ties, and many people in this part of the country know you." I felt as if the eyes of the world were staring at us as this dignified and successful man, this pillar of the community, bent down and picked up a dirty old penny. He then held up the coin as if to say, "It's all in a penny, elders; it's all in a penny." Then, he put the penny in his pocket.

Back then this point flew over my head. But his message worked on me for many years. Perhaps what this visionary man was attempting to teach me was to place value on the smallest measure of our monetary system. By so doing, the nickels, dimes, and quarters would be held in wiser hands. My dollars would not end up being sucked into a black hole or wind up on the endangered list, a far too common occurrence today. My posterity and I owe a great deal of gratitude to Oliver Davis of North Carolina. His life was a grand extension of the hand of God.

A penny is your bottom line. It is the brick from which all other monetary values are built. I liken a penny to a soldier. The more pennies you accumulate, the larger and more powerful your army's influence becomes. If you strategically deploy your forces, instead of constantly trading them off for depreciable products, these soldiers will work diligently around the clock to recruit new soldiers, even while you sleep. Every self-made millionaire understands and practices saving pennies and putting them to work. Ric Edelman explained,

> With those precious few remaining pennies, you decide to buy a soda with lunch. No big deal, you say. After all, it's only a dollar. Considering the huge amounts you're spending on taxes, homes, cars, clothes, insurance, food, and day care, what possible difference could one little dollar make? . . . Spending one dollar a day instead of investing it for forty years . . . translates to $190,000 that you won't have when you retire.[4]

If you think of pennies as your soldiers, parting with them is more difficult. Perhaps the next time you think of trading ten dollars for something you can do without, you will remember it's not just ten dollars. You are trading off a thousand soldiers who will never work for you again. You must ask yourself, "General, is it worth the casualties?"

Likewise, few of us get into trouble by making one or two foolish mistakes. Typically, we don't jump off the proverbial financial cliff in a single leap; we edge toward it a little here and a little there. Eventually we slip or are pushed off. One purchase at a time, people charge tens of thousands of dollars on their credit cards before they stop themselves and assess just how much they've spent. "It's easy," said my friend Kathy. "For years, if we saw something we wanted, we bought it and put it on a credit card, even if the interest rate was 20 percent or higher." One day she tallied up her credit-card balances. "How did we end up owing $20,000? Most of the money we sent in every month was just going to interest."

During my career, I transported some pretty extraordinary individuals. Therefore, my employer insisted I take my driving skills to a new and improved level. The intensive training I underwent taught me to forget much of what I knew about driving. I was taught it was ineffective to measure speed in terms of miles per hour, because accidents occur in much smaller increments. Instead, I was trained to calculate driving speed in terms of feet-per-second, by taking half of the mph rate and adding that number to the original mph. For example: 60 mph equals 90 feet per second. If a driver takes his eyes off the road for only 3 seconds while traveling at 60 mph, he will have traveled a distance of three basketball courts. A lot can happen within that distance, especially when you consider the driver's reaction time is another second—almost another basketball court length! Hence, unlike the masses who drive and think in terms of miles per hour, highly trained drivers are taught to think in feet-per-second, and the success is astounding. This simple formula and training instilled in my mind how important it is to always keep my eyes on the road. Most accidents could be prevented if everyone understood this information and put it into practice. It has always amazed me how a small adjustment in thinking can drastically change lives. In effect, many of us are traveling down the highway at a high rate of speed with our attention diverted.

Dynamite and the fifth amazing treasure enjoy striking similarities. Both deserve to be handled with care; both save countless hours of back-breaking labor, and both possess explosive capabilities. This treasure reveals:

We will advance considerably in our financial affairs when we stop measuring value in terms of dollar bills and view each dollar as one hundred penny soldiers. We will advance farther and faster when we view a hundred soldiers as commodities to save and put to work vs. something in our pocket to spend. Moreover, the masses will remain poor until they discover the enormous value and potential of each and every penny soldier. "The power of little things has so often been noted that we accept it as an axiom, and yet fail to see, in each beginning, the possibility of great events."[5]

The mighty Roman Empire was built one brick at a time. Happiness is achieved one kind deed at a time. Great accomplishments are composed of many little things done well. This point cannot be overstated. Again! The soundness of any financial foundation is the ability to capture and harness the value of a little copper penny. Perhaps you should ask yourself, general, what would Lincoln do? Unless you stand to inherit great wealth or possess rare talent, employed penny soldiers are your ticket to freedom and a better life.

Notes

1. "Bruce Barton quotes," http://www.quoteworld.org/quotes/1029.
2. Sam Walton, *Sam Walton, Made in America* (New York: Doubleday, 1992), 5.
3. Brigham Young, *Discourses of Brigham Young* (Salt Lake City: Deseret Book, 1978), 292.
4. Ric Edelman, *The New Rules of Money* (New York: HarperCollins, 1998), 13.
5. F. P. Edwards in *Richard Evans' Quote Book* (Salt Lake City: Publishers Press, 1971).

"And Cain loved Satan more than God . . . and slew Abel. And Cain said unto the lord: Satan tempted me because of my brother's flocks. And I was wroth." Moses 5:18, 38

Amazing Treasure Number Six

Focus on Needs: Backyard Goldmine!

Beyond question we live in perilous times. Today, evil manifests itself in many disguises. Materialism of Book of Mormon proportions infiltrates our homes and casts a dark, worrisome shadow upon our lives. Consumerism has a deep and hypnotic grip upon this nation. Our insatiable appetite for things has burdened us with trillions of dollars of unnecessary debt. Tragically our government has followed suit. Virtues have suffered and personal responsibilities have diminished. Foreclosures, bankruptcies, and broken homes are epidemic.

Due to the momentum of today's "need-to-have" propaganda and the pervasive doctrine that instant gratification is a right, our society throws caution to the wind. To our great detriment, we have ignored the future. To interrupt this process, the necessary adjustments may not be easy or happen overnight. There is no quick fix to remedy years of self-defeating behavior, accumulated debt, or poor money management. The good news is there is a fix.

My grandparents' generation endured the Great Depression and personally experienced the suffering, fear, and hunger that resulted from that long and uncertain period. Jobs were scarce and money was in short supply. Times were so harsh and lasted for such a protracted period that people from my grandparents' generation were never completely capable of forgetting the memories of that era. As a result, many people fostered a philosophy on handling money that was extremely effective, and they became one of the wealthiest generations in history. Sam Walton said, "No question about it, a lot of my attitude toward money stems from growing up during a pretty hardscrabble time in our country's history of the Great Depression."[1] In short, they came to understand how little they could survive on.

Uninterrupted years of economic growth and prosperity have caused much of this wisdom to be lost on my generation. Hence, Americans have amassed trillions upon trillions of dollars of personal debt. We bring all this tragedy and heartbreak upon us because we fail to bridle our wants.

Known for his wisdom and thrift, Benjamin Franklin understood the prudence which should govern our attitude about money, as well as the secret for achieving happiness:

> There are two ways of being happy: We may either diminish our wants or augment our means—either will do—the result is the same; and it is for each man to decide for himself, and do that which happens to be the easiest. If you are idle or sick or poor, however hard it may be to diminish your wants, it will be harder to augment your means. If you are active and prosperous or young or in good health, it may be easier for you to augment your means than to diminish your wants. But if you are wise, you will do both at the same time, young or old, rich or poor, sick or well; and if you are very wise you will do both in such a way as to augment the general happiness of society.[2]

The influence money has in our lives cannot be overstated; if used wisely it can be a wonderful blessing; if misused, it can become a curse. The love of money is one of Satan's most alluring and effective tools. He cleverly uses it to corrupt and lead the Lord's people into bondage. Our craving for material things has spiraled out of control to the point we have put our national security at risk. We scorn the federal government for compiling massive debt, and yet the collective debt of the private sector is even greater. The current mortgage crises, brought upon us in large measure by wide scale greed and overindulgence of both financial institutions and the consumer, has plunged our economy and financial markets into uncertainty and fear.

Howard W. Hunter said, "Latter-Day Saints have always been known as a frugal people; it is part of our history. . . . One of the greatest burdens we have had placed upon us and the thing that has taken more of our freedom than any other, perhaps, is indebtedness. Many of us become slaves to debt because we have failed to follow the recommendations of the authorities of the Church."[3]

So extreme is our thirst for more it has become a threat to the love and harmony of our homes. So compelling is our desire to keep up with others that we have been willing to ply the chains of bondage to make a good impression and show off our earthly spoils.

Self-help programs call postponing wants "delayed gratification." During this critical time, while we are setting our financial house in order, we must focus only on our life-sustaining needs, and we must employ delayed-gratification for our wants.

A woman told me a story about her daughter. The young woman, Ann, was fretting about her upcoming high school reunion. Understandably, Ann wanted to make her best impression on her former classmates. She hadn't seen most of them for ten years. Even though she and her husband were struggling to pay their current financial obligations, Ann shopped at fine clothing stores and charged expensive wardrobes for her and her husband to wear. Later in the week she pulled up to her mother's home in a new minivan. She rolled down the window and called out, "Oh mother, can you imagine the looks on their faces when they see me pull up in this?"

When she and her husband arrived at the high school reunion, awestruck spectators were not lined up at the sidewalk to greet them. A few couples were strolling around the grounds reminiscing. To Ann's dismay nobody paid any attention to her car or her clothing.

Were she and her husband being true to themselves by pretending a lifestyle beyond what they could afford? If they could not afford the vehicle, was buying it an indication of success or failure? They had blurred the line between wants and needs, and entered a danger zone. Over time, the purchase of this van led to much unhappiness for Ann and her husband. Consider this warning in 2 Nephi 9:51: "Do not spend money for that which is of no worth nor your labor for that which cannot satisfy."

How many of us have wished for a car, boat, or something so badly it actually made us miserable? "If I could only have this one thing I would be so happy," we tell ourselves. Yet, when we eventually obtain the possession, we lose interest and discard it a few weeks later. Thereafter, we reproduce the same scenario about something completely different to replicate the excitement.

Happiness cannot be bought on a store shelf; it must be earned. There is no income grand enough to satisfy the thirst of human want. Think of "wants" as the devil in the fine print. Needs, on the other hand, are the actual necessities of life. When we focus on needs, saving is spawned. Remember, happiness is achieved by living correct principles, serving and loving others, and actively pursuing worthy challenges and dreams. Happiness is never found in the pursuit of material things. "The more you have the more you want" is a destructive, selfish cycle that never ends. In the cycle, money (the means) becomes the end, and we begin searching for happiness in "that which hath no life" (Mormon 8:39). Money merely enhances happiness already achieved; it never creates it.

Unlike God, this world pays respect to wealth and many people cave to the materialistic mentality. If our home is large and situated high on a hill, society reinforces the notion that we have "arrived." In my profession, I used to drive beautiful corporate vehicles. I was amazed how generously the public reacted. Then I would drive home in my rusty old Dodge Colt and witness the contrasting reaction. We are not blind to this, and we sometimes yield to the temptation to gain others' admiration by what we own. We would be wise to remember that this prideful homage we seek is temporary and fleeting. If this is what we're searching for, we will always be found wanting. "He that loveth silver shall not be satisfied" (Ecclesiastes 5:10).

Why are so many rich people miserable? Perhaps they have fallen in love with something that can never return their love. They give it their full attention, but that attention is unrequited. I repeat this truism once again: happiness is achieved by living correct principles, serving and loving others, and actively pursuing worthy challenges and dreams.

There are those people of wealth who have found happiness through creating meaningful uses for their money. We applaud them. But far too many wealthy individuals end up with broken lives. Lost and lonely, surrounded by wealth and superficial friends they have bought, they embark on an endless search for happiness—usually by trying to accumulate more wealth or by using drugs or alcohol to temporarily ease the loneliness and pain.

Consider that life's excitements are found in the anticipating, the pursuit, not necessarily the attainment of the dream. The weeks preceding Christmas are much more exciting than the actual day. Most gifts are relegated to the closet within days. Perhaps one of the reasons some wealthy people are unhappy is because they lack the anticipation of a dream. If they want something, they just buy it. Where's the challenge? Where's the satisfaction? But for those of us who must stretch to provide needs, wants can work to our benefit. They can provide us an opportunity to dream, plan, and work hard. But they can also be destructive if planning, patience, and caution are not applied. John Ruskin effectively describes the futility and madness of the uncontrolled thirst for more:

> I dreamed that I was at a child's party, in which every means of entertainment had been provided by a wise and kind host. The children had been set free in the rooms and gardens, with no care whatever but how to pass their afternoon rejoicingly. There was music, all manner of amusing books, a workshop, a table loaded with everything nice to eat, and whatever a child could fancy, but in the midst of all this it struck two or three of the more "practical" children that they would like some of the brass-headed nails that studded the chairs, and so they set to work to pull them out. In a little while all the children, nearly, were spraining their fingers in pulling out brass-headed nails. With all that they could pull out they were not satisfied; and then everybody wanted some of somebody else's. And at last the really "practical" and "sensible" ones declared that nothing was of any real consequence that afternoon except to get plenty of brass-headed nails. And at last they began to fight for nail heads, even though they knew they would not be allowed to carry so much as one brass knob away with them. But no! It was "Who has the most nails? I must have as many as you before I leave the house or I cannot possibly go home in peace." At last they made so much noise that I awoke and thought to myself, "What a false dream that is of children. Children never do such foolish things. Only men do."[4]

How many of Gods' children miss out on the Master Host's lavish party by the tenacious pursuit of brass nails? Likewise, how many of us miss out on the grand party of life in the frantic pursuit of green paper, sparkling stones, and many other items we do not really need? N. Eldon Tanner shared the following story about President Hugh B. Brown:

> As a young soldier in World War I, he was visiting an elderly friend in the hospital. This friend was a millionaire several times over who, at the age of eighty, was lying at death's door. Neither his divorced wife nor any of his five children cared enough to come to the hospital to see him. As President Brown thought of the things his friend "had lost which money could not buy and noted his tragic situation and the depth of his misery," he asked his friend how he would change the course of his life if he had it to live over again.

> The old gentleman, who died a few days later, said: "As I think back over my life the most important and valuable asset which I might have had but which I lost in the process of accumulating my millions, *was the simple faith my mother had in God and in the immortality of the soul.*"
>
> You asked me what is the most valuable thing in life. I cannot answer you in better words than those used by the poet. He asked President Brown to get a little book out of his briefcase from which he read a poem entitled "I'm an Alien."
>
> I'm an alien, to the faith my mother taught me.
> I'm a stranger to the God that heard my mother when she cried.
> I'm an alien to the comfort that, "Now I lay me," brought me.
> To the everlasting arms that held my father when he died.
> When the great world came and called me, I deserted all to follow.
> Never noting in my blindness I had slipped my hand from His.
> Never dreaming in my dazedness that the bubble fame is hollow.
> That the wealth of gold is tinsel, as I since have learned it is.
> I have spent a lifetime seeking things I spurned when I found them,
> I have fought and been rewarded in many a winning cause,
> But I'd give it all, fame and fortune and the pleasures that surround them,
> If I only had the faith *that made my mother what she was.*[5]

Anytime you step into a store, you are stepping into a finely tuned selling machine. Everything is designed to bring you to the point of purchase. It doesn't matter what you buy, so long as you buy something. So, in addition to getting what you came for, this selling machine especially wants to capitalize on your tendency to buy something else on impulse. Media advertising combines ideas of popularity, happiness, and fun with the purchase of products. Behind the scenes, before you ever see the ads, they have spent exhaustive time and money researching how you will react. They know what to stock and where to place it to stimulate your urge to buy. "The purpose of most mass media is to work a long-term, cumulative change in images and perceptions of a given product. They do not [only] intend the Lexus ads to persuade some wealthy, middle-aged consumer to go out and buy the car as soon as possible, but they are also designed to plant the idea in younger viewers that this automobile is a desirable status symbol, a suitable trophy to crown future success."[6]

In her article, "When Men Put on Appearances," Diane Barthel explains how the media attempts to influence men: "In car ads the words power, precision and performance are used to appeal to a predominantly male audience. Sometimes the car is a woman, more pliant and responsive than any real woman. The advertising world strives to control the buying power of consumers. They influence everything from alcohol to deodorant to male bonding and how to choose a Scotch to impress your dad."[7]

Other advertising efforts target women, young adults, children, and senior citizens in all geographic and economic brackets. Millions of research dollars are spent each year to affect sales of products and services. Is it any wonder we walk around in a constant state of "purchase neurosis"? Our minds have been cleverly programmed to buy. Like being an alcoholic, consumer addicts are growing in number. It can become a disease every bit as destructive as substance abuse.

On a lighter note, I am reminded of the elderly English woman pushing a shopping cart.

She is met by a friend, who peers in the cart and asks, "What you got there, Mrs. Robinson?"

Nonchalantly, Mrs. Robinson replies, "A V-8 piston engine."

Confused at the sight of this big motor in her friend's cart, the friend asks, "Why did you buy it?"

Mrs. Robinson replies, "Cause it was a bargain!" How often do we fill our garages and basements with piston engine type things we don't need or will probably never use?

Advertising moguls have discovered humans can be conditioned to buy from carefully tailored stimuli. Understanding the motives and the science behind advertising can help you to avoid the trap. Children are particularly vulnerable to media advertising, which might be another reason to limit television viewing time In fact, a recent study concluded that children preferred hamburgers packaged in McDonalds wrapping over other identical burgers in other packaging.

Happiness despises children who get everything they want and adults who want what they cannot have. To some degree, it is healthy for children to be left wanting. Resist the temptation of giving children everything their little hearts desire. A child who has his every want satisfied will surely become spoiled. There is wisdom in the philosophy that reasonably deprived children produce exceptional adults. I admire several well-to-do parents who moved their families back into modest neighborhoods so they could keep their children's feet planted firmly on the ground.

We must cultivate the ability to discern wants from needs. Once we have differentiated between the two, our wants must be reigned in and put into cold storage for a season. Remember, too, that uncontrolled want will poison your heart and rob you of peace. As Albert Schweitzer said, "I don't know what your destiny will be, but one thing I know: the only ones among you who will be really happy are those who have sought and found how to serve."[8]

When I want something badly and I am trying to determine if it is a need or want, I ask myself: "Is it something I really need? Can I do without it for a few years? Would the money be better applied to something else (credit card debt, the mortgage)?" Last but not least, I ask: "Would having it mean as much to me if everyone in the world was blind?" I take pride in being able to tell myself "no" or "not now;" often the acquisition will be much sweeter down the road after I've built a solid foundation. When want begins to occupy my thoughts too frequently, I retreat to a quiet place to pray and meditate. I remind myself it's not about having what I want. It's about wanting what I have. Rich is the individual who understands the value of the present, knows where to apply it and does not squander it foolishly.

The cure for unbridled want is to recognize that of all earthly commodities, time, not material things, reigns supreme. What we trade it for will largely determine our happiness, who we become and where we ultimately end up. Regarding the time which composes a man's life Jesus taught, "Greater love hath no man than he who lays down his life for a friend" (John 15:13). This scripture is as much about laying down *time* in the service of a friend as it is about actually dying for him. Either way he gives the ultimate sacrifice.

Legend has it that long, long ago a thunderous lightning bolt stuck at the foot of a wise man. When the smoke and fire cooled, a priceless jewel emerged and he called it the sixth amazing treasure:

Too many people trade away their precious future for things which rust, rot, and decay. When we draw our last breath, we will not think of one solitary worldly possession we have acquired, but rather we will have a deep and abiding concern for our loved ones. Did we love them enough? Did we spend enough time with them? Will the time we spent together sustain them through life's many difficulties? It has been overstated that time is money. But this is only partially true; money cannot add one more moment to your life when the final curtain closes. When the end comes, how many of us will be willing to gladly give everything we own for one more day—one more hour?

Notes

1. Sam Walton, *Sam Walton, Made in America* (New York: Doubleday, 1992), 3.
2. Benjamin Franklin, "Health Quotations," http://www.futurehealth.org/healthqu.htm
3. Howard W. Hunter, "Economics and Welfare Principles," *The Teachings of Howard W. Hunter* (Salt Lake City: Bookcraft, 2002), 159.
4. John Ruskin in *Richard Evans' Quote Book* (Salt Lake City: Publishers Press, 1971).
5. N. Eldon Tanner, "Constancy Amid Change," *Ensign*, Nov. 1979, 80. (italics in original)
6. Michael Medved, *Hollywood vs. America* (New York: HarperCollins, 1992), xxiii.
7. Diane Barthel, "When Men Put on Appearances," *Men, Masculinity and Media*, ed. Steve Craig (London: SAGE, 1992), 137-153.
8. "Albert Schweitzer quotes," http://www.brainyquote.com/quotes/quotes/a/albertschw133001.html.

"I learned about the strength you can get from a close family life. I learned to keep going, even in bad times. I learned not to despair, even when my world was falling apart. I learned that there are no free lunches. And I learned the value of hard work. In the end, you've got to be productive. That's what made this country great—and that's what's going to make us great again." —Lee Iaccoca[1]

Amazing Treasure Number Seven

The Big Guns of Resourcefulness!

In his book entitled *1001 Ways to Cut Your Expenses*, Jonathan Pond lists examples of how to save money. Some of his methods are clever. One example is: "Buy a goat. It mows your lawn, gives milk, cheese, and possibly meat."[2] Although lists of money-saving ideas can be valuable, I prefer to teach correct money-management principles. The Prophet Joseph suggested that arming people with correct principles puts them in a position to govern themselves. I'll teach you the principles and you can make your own list of specific ways to save.

When I received my patriarchal blessing, the wise old patriarch gathered my large family around him to share some profound truths he had learned in his life. One in particular stands out. When he and his sweetheart married, they could only afford to live in an old chicken coop that belonged to his father-in-law. He and his new bride had to clean it out in order to have a roof over their heads. He said, "Of all the lovely places we lived, we were never happier than during those years we lived in a chicken coop." Then he turned to me and said, "Young man, it is amazing what you can accomplish if you're willing to start at the bottom and pay the price." That day he taught me resourceful people think of alternatives, and they are unconventional when occasion requires.

Due to a few bad breaks in his life, my father never made much money. His tenth child was born during the early 1970s at a time when he was making less than four dollars an hour. Out of sheer desperation, my parents had to be resourceful. One of my childhood memories is watching my father repair things. He could fix almost anything: appliances, furnaces, automobiles, and television sets. My father repaired whatever broke down. When our old car's transmission went out, he pulled out the owner's manual and began to tear it apart. He stuck with it until he understood how everything worked. I never remember seeing a repairman come to our home. My father could even sew as well as my mother and often helped my sisters sew dresses. He carpeted two bedrooms in our home with discarded carpet samples by meticulously cutting the pieces and gluing them together in a giant puzzle. We lovingly called them our carpets of many colors. The carpets endured our large family for many years. My father did the household plumbing and electrical work. He took the bus to work every day to save gas and to cut down on the wear and tear on our twenty-year-old station wagon. He even set the broken bones of animals. He had an extensive knowledge of herbs and remedies to help us when we were sick. Seldom was it necessary for any of us to visit a doctor. He did whatever was necessary to make ends meet. He improvised, adapted, and overcame. Mostly my dear father worked hard and was willing to go without.

To this day I am uncertain how my mother handled her large family's needs with father's humble paycheck. She performed daily miracles. She understood the value of every dollar and how to get the most from it. She walked or took the bus most everywhere she went. She shopped clearance sales. Somehow her children were always dressed nicely. She cooked from scratch and purchased food in large quantities. My mother budgeted so we could survive on a shoestring, and she seemed to squeeze water from rocks.

A sewer rat is a clever and resourceful animal. He is a scrapper, a survivor, and a highly adaptive creature. He knows his surroundings well and makes the most of his environment. A sewer rat is a problem solver. If he can't climb over an obstacle, he finds an alternate path or tunnels through it. He doesn't whine about his difficult life. Due to the adverse conditions and extremities that surround him, he has become largely immune to diseases. The adversity in his life has made him strong and adaptive. Out of necessity, he has developed independence and an unconquerable will.

The sewer rat's spoiled white cousin, the domestic rat, on the other hand, is an entirely different creature. The white rat approaches problems with little or no resolve. Coddled and accustomed to the good life, it will lie down and die if food and water aren't laid before it daily.

Several years ago, a friend and I had to work late. Toward the end of our project he asked me for a ride home. I told him he was more than welcome to ride home with me in my personal stretch limousine—the bus. Perplexed, he reluctantly agreed.

On our fifty-minute ride home, the last bus out of town on a Friday night was filled with drunks, druggies, and other interesting characters. My friend scooted closer and closer to me as they filled in at every stop. On one particular stop, several men with long, unkempt hair, wearing black, ragged clothes boarded the bus. Under his breath my friend said, "Oh, this is just great." The face of the group's leader was gaunt, and it looked as if it was the skull of a dead man. As he passed by, he said in a friendly tone, "Oh hi, Jeff, how ya been?" and I replied, "Fine, Spider, it's been a while." My friend noticeably relaxed. Later, he whispered he couldn't believe Spider and I were on a first-name basis. My friend, like the domestic rat, had never had to adapt. Although he could have saved a lot of money and wear and tear on his vehicle, I never saw him on a bus again.

There is power and magic in being resourceful. Like the sewer rat, resourceful people have a way of making things happen. They do a lot with very little. Their self-talk is forward and positive; and they believe in themselves. Maintaining a positive attitude is essential to success. Charles Swindoll said,

> The longer I live, the more I realize the impact of attitude on life. Attitude to me, is more important than facts. It is more important than the past, than education, than money, than circumstances, than failures, than successes, than what other people think or say or do. It will make or break a company, . . . a church, . . . a home. The remarkable thing is we have a choice every day regarding the attitude we will embrace for that day. We cannot change the past. . . . We cannot change the fact that people will act a certain way. We cannot change the inevitable. The only thing we can do is play on the one string we have, and that is our attitude. . . . I am convinced that life is ten percent what happens to me and ninety percent how I react to it. And so it is with you. . . . We are in charge of our attitudes.[3]

Truly resourceful individuals have a magnetic field around them that attracts positive elements wherever they go. Doors open for them; and deals appear to fall into their laps. When they are knocked down they get up, brush themselves off, and continue forward. More than luck, I believe this phenomenon is the result of can-do, positive thinking.

Therefore, stay positive, develop your talents, multiply your skills, and good things will begin to happen—exponentially. Becoming resourceful involves time and commitment. Cultivate a desire to take control, become independent, and be curious about how things work, become good with your hands, and gain a working knowledge of various trades and their respective tools. Ask experts a lot of questions. This will assist you in gaining a wide range of knowledge and in becoming versatile. A trademark of effective executives is that they ask a lot of questions. Knowledge begets knowledge, success begets success; and the better part of luck is attracted to a moving, thinking target.

With all the complexities and expenses of today's world, we need to be able to approach it in many ways. Becoming truly resourceful is one of the best ways to drastically cut expenses and expand one's reach. In my case, I merely imitated the skills of my parents and, almost magically, money began to accumulate.

The seventh amazing treasure burns as a flaming torch of eternal truth. It states:

The intricate and daily exercise of resourcefulness in our lives makes us capable of devising a way and means, an ability to meet and navigate difficult situations. Resourcefulness ably serves as a cistern to catch and preserve the wealth from life's overflowing cup. Lord, give me a few sticks, and life and I will make some happiness.

Notes

1. Lee Iacocca with William Novak, *Iacocca: An Autobiography* (New York: Bantam, 1984).
2. Jonathan D. Pond, *1001 Ways to Cut Your Expenses* (New York: Dell, 1992).
3. "Charles Swindoll quotes," http://thinkexist.com/quotation/the_longer_i_live-the_more_i_realize_the_impact/296740.html.

"The heights by great men reached and kept
Were not attained by sudden flight,
But they, while their companions slept,
Were toiling upward in the night."
—Henry W. Longfellow[1]

Amazing Treasure Number Eight

Safety in Numbers? Thinking Outside The Herd

Although others can cheer him on, it is the Olympiad who must prepare himself to one day enter the stadium. Few noteworthy accomplishments are achieved in the midst of the crowd. Most of my education was obtained studying at a desk in a quiet corner. My wife and I bucked current trends by paying off our debts, and one penny at a time built a solid financial foundation. Much of the information in this book was formulated during quiet mornings and evenings. We are taught that even salvation must be accomplished alone. A man cannot think outside the herd unless occasionally and effectively he separates himself from the safety and influence of the crowd.

As we passed the mall, practically everyone on the bus was straining to catch a glimpse. There she was dancing to her headset like an awkward performer on a stage. Completely oblivious to the gathering spectators, the young woman vigorously expressed herself in a way most would not associate with beautiful dancing. You see, she was handicapped and that made moving fluidly difficult. Unlike the busloads of onlookers with gloomy, morning work faces, she was obviously happy. Though she danced her dance of life alone at 7:00 AM on a Monday morning, she taught me all over again what it means to walk to the beat of your own drummer. What she was doing not only took courage but a strong dose of crowd-crushing individuality. "But ye are a chosen generation, a royal priesthood, an holy nation, a peculiar people" (1 Peter 2:9).

I recently saw a cartoon depicting a herd of sheep lazily grazing in a field. One of the sheep was standing on his two back hooves in the middle of the herd crying loudly, "Listen! Please! Listen to me! If we put our minds to it we can be so much more than people." I remember a similar scene in the halls of my high school many years ago. Several boys were leaning against a wall in between classes and poking fun at others who were different from them. In a twisted understanding of individuality each had a similar haircut, each sported a pullover T-shirt, each wore Levi's brand pants, and white Converse tennis shoes. As a studious boy passed by, dressed differently, a member of the group laughed and called him a conformist.

Humans tend to not only follow the herd, but also pressure unlike minds to conform to the group as well. Frankly speaking, this can be hazardous to our happiness and financial wellness.

I learned this at a young age. I was bussed to a school located in an affluent area of town. Many students drove nice cars given to them by well-to-do parents. They wore only the finest name-brand clothing. Popularity seemed linked to family financial status and mine scraped the bottom of the barrel. By the time I graduated from high school, I realized I had benefited from those sometimes long and lonely years.

Perhaps my most interesting discovery from this difficult era was the enormous void I found in the hearts of countless young people, each yearning to be accepted and understood by their peers. I was pleasantly surprised to find a few well-adjusted, well-coached youth who, with a modest investment and a kind word or two, broke away from the crowd, reached out, and freed individuals from the psychological scars and limitations that had been placed upon them by others.

I read once that most adult insecurities originate in youth. Think for a moment of the social ills that could be virtually eliminated if parents actively and assertively taught their children to think outside the herd and be more accepting. Almost overnight the broad use of anti-depressant drugs would taper off to an insignificant dribble. Social afflictions like drug addictions, alcoholism, bulimia, and anorexia would be reduced from their now epidemic proportions. With more of our children loved and included, we would have less violent crimes acted out on society like the mass killings in shopping malls and schools. Should we continue to allow our children to segregate into "popular" or "unpopular" groups? This is cruel and unhealthy, and the situation desperately needs serious parental intervention.

When I was young, my friends and I liked to tease an unusual boy named Stephen. A year older than my friends and me, Stephen was an outsider and very different from us. He was an easy target for ridicule. He was reserved, tall and lanky, and wore thick-rimmed glasses. We aggravated him to the point of tears and chased him all over the schoolyard. Then one day Stephen moved from the neighborhood. Only years later would our paths cross again. I was sitting on a bus en route to work when I looked up and saw Stephen toward the front of the bus. My heart sank as I remembered how I had treated him. He seemed to have changed very little; he sat alone. After a few minutes, I gathered my belongings and moved to the front of the bus and sat down next to Stephen. "Hi, I'm Jeffrey Hair," I said. "Do you remember me?"

"Oh yeah," Stephen replied, "how could I ever forget you."

Nervously I continued, "This may sound lame and insincere, but my friends and I treated you badly and I am so very sorry. I have thought about you through the years and have wished I could do it all over again. Can you find it in your heart to forgive me?"

To my surprise Stephen was pleasant and asked me not to worry another moment; he had forgiven my friends and me. He then asked what I did for a living. I told him I provided protection for dignitaries. He smiled and said, "You picked a good job for your skills." We both laughed freely.

"What is your vocation, Stephen?" I asked.

Without hesitation, he reached into his pocket, pulled out a card, wrote something on it, and handed it to me. "I am a shoe shiner at a local department store," he said, "and would like to give you this coupon for a free shoe shine."

I felt my heart tear. Here was this good man whom I had teased relentlessly now offering me a special gift. I doubted I was capable of a more genuine display of humility. He was willing to shine the shoes of the person who had made life so difficult for him!

As we parted, I pondered what life might have been like for Stephen had we opened our arms to him and been more accepting. Of course, shining shoes is an honorable profession. However, I am absolutely certain Stephen could have accomplished anything had he received more positive support. I never made good on the coupon from Stephen. His simple little card was too valuable for me to part with. And, I suppose I did not feel deserving of such a special honor. May God bless you, Stephen; you are a much better man than I am. You would be proud to know I have since learned true wealth and happiness is found in building, loving, and encouraging, and not in tearing down.

Despite my difficult high school experience, I, too, learned to eventually accept and like myself. I understood and appreciated my uniqueness and began accepting others for theirs. The skill of being able to think on my own and shed myself of peer pressure had taken root in my young life. I learned to make decisions objectively. I found the courage to act independently and stand up to be counted when the situation warranted.

Learning to think outside the herd regarding monetary matters and strategies is also critical. According to statistics, very few save money, and consumer debt is commonplace.

Someone once said: "The journey of discovery lies not in seeking new vistas, but in seeing with new eyes." One day I was driving with my fourteen-year-old son, Andrew, and his friend, Philip. The boys had recently begun to discover the opposite sex but were still stubbornly unwilling to admit it. We had just passed a dance hall where a dozen girls were standing in front, scantily dressed. I noticed both boys' heads turned to take a look as we passed by. After a few moments, I asked them what they had been staring at. "Oh nothing," they nervously responded. I revealed I had seen them sneaking a peak. Turning various shades of red, they both vehemently denied it. As I continued my interrogation, my son's friend finally blurted, "It's not me. It's these eyes!"

Benjamin Franklin cleverly observed, "The eyes of other people are the eyes that ruin us. If all but myself were blind, I should want neither fine clothes, fine houses, nor fine furniture."

Recently a man requested advice for his failing marriage. As his story developed, he proudly explained his family lived on a hill in a big home; he drove nice cars, and overall, enjoyed the good life. He seemed very pleased that he and his wife had the respect of family, friends, and business associates. However, this lifestyle had an expensive price tag. He had to work sixty-plus hours a week, yet financially they were *still* slowly going in the hole. According to his own admission, the time away from home was taking its toll on his marriage. The simple answer was obvious: cut back on the lifestyle and spend more time with his wife and family. But he could not get past the idea that his friends and family would think he was a failure. Apparently this consideration was more important than saving his marriage. "There is no act however trivial, but has its train of consequences."[3]

In order to achieve our potential and get where we want to be, we must rethink failed strategies. That requires us to elevate ourselves above others and stop the habit of accumulating things merely to impress. Although I wouldn't recommend it, wouldn't it be a different world if we had our true net worth daily stamped on our foreheads? Would our priorities change drastically?

I cannot emphasize enough the importance of getting off the beaten path. Lehi's dream affirms the fact there is no safety in moving with the crowd. Instead of throwing precious resources down a never-ending pit in a futile effort to be accepted, we can develop and follow an effective individual strategy. By thinking outside the herd, we can enjoy each other's unique qualities, the delicious feast, and the atmosphere of the party. It is here we can achieve our greatest happiness and financial possibilities. We need not worry about losing friends because true friends and God will be there for us when the dust settles. As a matter of fact, it will be comforting to discover who they really are. "If ye were of the world, the world would love his own: but because ye are not of the world, but I have chosen you out of the world, therefore the world hateth you" (John 15:19).

In the final analysis, we must develop the internal fortitude to act independently of the opinions of others. In order to rise to our God-given potential and make the necessary tough decisions which will lead us to our highest vistas, we must at times be willing to walk alone—beyond the lighted path.

Beneath the surface of the unsightly cocoon, the eighth amazing treasure bursts forth as an elegant butterfly. The treasure proclaims:

Go therefore and be thyself along life's byways. Spend only a precious little time blending in, for you were created to stand out. Remember to rejoice in the uniqueness of others and always leave them better than you found them. In the end you will discover a man's height is not determined as much by material possessions as it is by what he does with them. For "it is easy in the world to live after the world's opinions; it is easy in solitude to live after our own; but the great man is he who in the midst of the crowd keeps with perfect sweetness the independence of solitude."[4]

Notes

1. "Henry W. Longfellow" http://en.wikiquote.org/wiki/Henry_W._Longfellow.
2. Benjamin Franklin, *Life of Benjamin Franklin* (Baltimore: Lippincott, 1875), 279.
3. "Character by Samuel Smiles," http://virtuescience.com/samuel-smiles.html.
4. "Ralph Waldo Emerson quotes," http://thinkexist.com/quotation/it_is_easy_in_the_world_to_live_after_the_world-s/157874.html.

"While the earth remaineth, seedtime and harvest . . . shall not cease."
Genesis: 8:22

Amazing Treasure Number Nine

The Law of the Harvest

In properly prepared soil, we can reasonably expect that every seed we sow will someday yield fruit. If we skip the steps of soil preparation and planting seeds, there can be little harvest. However, we can count on weeds springing up everywhere.

The law of the harvest is an order that must be followed to be successful. The laws of nature cannot be circumvented. We must work in harmony with these laws. If we plant seeds of wheat, we will harvest wheat. If we plant good seeds we will harvest good fruit; and if we plant bad seeds we will harvest bad fruit. Good seeds will not produce bad fruit; and bad seeds will not produce good fruit. Therefore, we must be anxiously engaged in planting many good seeds as early in our lives as possible. We must get an education, develop good habits, work hard, and wisely use our limited resources. The life of Lehi's son Nephi typifies the power and potential of the law of the harvest. Nephi was called by the Lord to leave the riches and comfort of his father's house and enter into the wilderness for a time and a season. Here, a young and inexperienced Nephi not only had to contend with extreme elements of the desert and ocean but with his rebellious brothers as well. In addition, he learned to follow instructions, work with metals, build a ship, and cross an ocean, as well as help guide his people. Along the way, his father and the Lord taught him many true principles and skills. By the time he arrived in the new world, Nephi had paid the price and transformed himself from a youth to a wise and skillful leader. Under his direction his rather insignificant band of travelers became a mighty and industrious people.

Ideally, soil preparation and seed planting should occur in the springtime of our lives. What happens when seeds are planted in the summer or fall? What kind of yield should we expect? The law of the harvest suggests the optimum time for individuals to prepare the soil of their financial future is during those critical years before and immediately after marriage. If this time is wasted, it will be difficult to compensate for the loss.

The law of the harvest involves delayed gratification. The law of the harvest suggests that attempting to reap in the spring will cause serious consequences. What would happen to a farmer who carelessly used up or mishandled his next year's planting seeds? This is exactly what many young people do when they make major, unnecessary purchases. It is now the trend for young married couples to have two cars and a nice apartment. Too often, they run up credit cards and personal debt as they squander this most critical time with personal indulgences. If only they understood the laws that govern the harvest and utilized their precious springtime to prepare the soil and sew seeds for the future.

> Every generation a new crop of fools comes on. They think they can beat the orderly universe. They conceive themselves to be more clever than the eternal laws. They snatch goods from Nature's counter, and pay—pay in tears, in agony, in despair; pay as fools before them have paid. . . . Nature keeps books pitilessly. Your credit with her is good, but she collects; there is no land you can flee to and escape her bailiffs. . . . She never forgets; she sees to it that you pay her every cent you owe, with interest.[1]

The law of the harvest requires sacrificing the material things we want now in order to secure an abundant tomorrow. The reckless, debt-driven approach to life will yield only weeds of heartache and premature worrying and aging.

The law of the harvest purports that a good education comes before acquiring luxuries. During the preparatory years, we should live conservatively. For example, if you can possibly arrange to do so, take the bus. If that is not possible, drive a reliable, modest car. Upon completion of the preparatory years, the law of the harvest suggests carefully purchasing a modest home should come before expensive automobiles or indulging in expensive entertainment or hobbies. Today divorce is too common, and the greatest cause is finance. Pogo said it this way, "We have met the enemy and he is us."[2]

Last but not least, the eternal law of the harvest requires us to place God and His ways ahead of seeking the riches of the earth: "But before ye seek for riches, seek ye for the kingdom of God. And after ye have obtained a hope in Christ ye shall obtain riches, if ye seek them; and ye will seek them for the intent to do good—to clothe the naked, and to feed the hungry, and to liberate the captive, and administer relief to the sick and the afflicted" (Jacob 2:18–19). True joy and wealth requires us to align our lives with eternal law and order as prescribed by God. Man's unhappiness can generally be traced to his attempts to rearrange or alter these heavenly guidelines. Efforts to dismiss them as not applicable or old-fashioned will lead us to great peril. May we have the wisdom to understand and work in harmony with the everlasting law of the harvest and the resulting happiness it will shed upon us.

Hence, the ninth Amazing Treasure is as rich as earth's most dark and fertile soil. It sets forth this truth:

Understanding and working in harmony with the law of the harvest will bring order and yield in our lives. "To every thing there is a season, and a time to every purpose under the heaven: A time to be born, and a time to die; a time to plant, and time to pluck up that which is planted" (Ecclesiastes 3:1–3). Furthermore, "There is a law, irrevocably decreed in heaven before the foundations of the world, upon which all blessings are predicated. And when we obtain any blessing from God, it is by obedience to that law upon which it is predicated" (D&C 130:20–21). Preparation and obedience to God's laws are the fulcrums for all true success. A bountiful harvest in the fall of life will depend upon springtime preparation.

Notes

1. Dr. Frank Crane, as quoted in "The Inferior Man," http://psychjourney_blogs.typepad.com/bohdi_sanders/2008/07/the-inferior-ma.html.
2. "Pogo quotes," http://igopogo.com/final_authority.htm.

"All the good things of the world are no further good to us than as they are of use, and of all we may heap up we enjoy only as much as we can use, and no more." —Daniel Defoe[1]

Amazing Treasure Number Ten

Frugality & Thrift: The Wise Man's Money Magnet

Without frugality and thrift, anything goes until everything is lost. My grandmother was the personification of frugality. Nothing was wasted under her jurisdiction. A product of the Great Depression, she was never informed when the frugality of that era ended. Of all the important people I have had the privilege of knowing, none had anything up on my grandmother regarding her understanding and application of the principles of thrift and frugality.

Many summers ago, my younger brother and I had the opportunity of staying with my grandmother and helping her around the farm. Living in an isolated farming community, my grandmother learned to be independent. Her pantries were always stocked to the brim with various grains, and dried, bottled, and canned foods. Several cords of firewood lined the outside wall of the cellar. I am convinced that if the economy entirely collapsed, my grandmother could have continued to live comfortably.

Grandma always had a large garden and practically lived off its yield year-round. In my grandmother's world everything was saved and anything that wasn't saved was fed to the chickens and goats. What the chickens and goats wouldn't eat was put on the compost pile for next year's garden. Even the eggshells were crushed and recycled to the chickens.

Meals with grandma consisted of fresh eggs and goat's milk, homemade wheat bread, cottage cheese and yogurt, and home-grown meat and vegetables. Because the bread had no preservatives, my grandmother would store it in the freezer. If I wanted a slice of bread, I cut a piece off the frozen loaf with a special knife, and then I toasted it in the oven. It was delicious.

Grandma made her food the old-fashioned way, from scratch. When my grandmother purchased a pot or pan, she used it until it had worn so thin a hole developed. If possible she would then find another use for it. She was a woman of industry and thrift. She literally lived the old proverb, "Use it up, wear it out, make it do, or do without."

My grandmother was prepared and her resources were deep. After her death, her children found a substantial amount of silver hidden in her cellar and several savings accounts across the country with sizable amounts of money in each.

President Kimball would have loved my grandmother; they were slices off the same loaf. Concerning food storage, the importance of planting gardens, and living frugally, he said:

> We encourage you to grow all the food that you feasibly can on your own property. Berry bushes, grapevines, fruit trees—plant them if your climate is right for their growth. Grow vegetables and eat them from your own yard. Even those residing in apartments or condominiums can generally grow a little food in pots and planters. Study the best methods of providing your own food, make your garden as neat and attractive as well as productive. If there are children in your home, involve them in the process with assigned responsibilities.
>
> Wherever possible, produce your nonfood necessities of life. Improve your sewing skills; sew and mend clothing for your family. All the girls want to learn to type, they all want to go to an office. They don't seem to want to sew anymore, and to grow and protect and renew the things that they use. Develop handicraft skills . . . and make or build needed items.[2]

A young man who was financially struggling approached a friend of mine and asked how he had done so well raising his large family on such a meager income. My friend began to explain the principle of frugality when the fellow abruptly interrupted, "Things are so tough now and we only have one child. What will it be like when we have two or three? Already we've had to cut our nights out from five to three."

Brigham Young taught the early Saints if they weren't careful, a woman could throw out more with a spoon than a man could bring in with a shovel.[3] That was the beauty of my grandmother's ways—she made the most of every stroke of my grandfather's shovel. If a man wishes to see waste, he need look no further than his own home or local restaurants. Landfills across the country are overflowing with our waste. How much food is tossed from our tables and refrigerators that could be utilized with a little extra planning? My father taught us children that if we wanted the Lord's blessings, we should never waste what He has been kind enough to give us.

When we were starting out, my family received a few boxes of used clothing from relatives. Pleased, we set about selecting what we could use and sent the remainder to a large, struggling family. The mother refused the boxes and proudly stated, "My children will never wear secondhand clothing." Apparently, her door of frugality was closed.

Frugality requires we set aside our pride and, with a grateful heart, accept and utilize the blessings that come our way. I am intrigued that some of the wealthiest people I know shop at yard sales and thrift stores. They have learned something the middleclass should learn. It has been aptly stated that we can be our own worst enemy.

One day I was running some errands for a friend. I had just parked his car and was entering a home improvement store. A man approached me and asked about the well-kept corporate vehicle I was driving. He was so impressed he wanted to know the make and year. I did not tell him the owner was an important dignitary, but I was proud to announce it was a several-year-old Ford sedan. It had been well maintained to keep its beauty. Years later, when the car was replaced, the owner would not allow the purchase of a new vehicle—it had to be used.

On another occasion this same dignitary came to me with an armful of white shirts and said, "Jeff, you look about my size, would you be interested in some shirts that still have some good life left in them?" What do you think my answer was? He also knew I liked to weld, and on numerous occasions brought me stacks of hangers he saved from the dry cleaners. These hangers made exceptional welding rods. This shrewd and powerful CEO was value-conscious, frugal, and never lost sight of the value of big or little things.

How fortunate that the Old Testament Egyptians listened to Joseph and prepared for hard times during the seven years of prosperity. What significance does this story have in our lives? What are the prophets telling us today? Are we listening? Brigham Young once said, "If you are without bread, how much wisdom can you boast, and of what real utility are your talents, if you cannot procure for yourselves and save against a day of scarcity those substances designed to sustain your natural lives."[4]

If you waste not, you will want not. Wisdom dictates we should employ frugality and thrift as the honored watchmen in our financial tower and the feared enemies of debt and materialism will flea and never overtake us.

In the critical battle of life, living prudently can prevent us from being overtaken by misfortune. The judicious marshalling of our limited assets reduces waste and puts more penny soldiers at our command. Tragically, frugality and thrift have a negative stigma today. At our own peril, we poke fun and turn the tables on these powerful virtues. We hear them equated with being tight and selfish. We mindlessly dismiss them as old-fashioned.

Unlike my grandmother and the extraordinary dignitaries I have come to know, spendthrifts are a dime a dozen. However, the disciplined are in great demand and are rare indeed. People achieve greatness because they cultivate and practice great traits and characteristics. Interwoven in their lives, one is sure to find the highly uncommon virtues of thrift and frugality. No finer blessing can visit a home or nation than these two honorable qualities, for under their guidance abundance flourishes and peace reigns supreme.

Wherefore, the tenth amazing treasure possesses the efficiency of a seafaring schooner with the relentless and mighty trade winds at the back of its sails. The treasure boldly decrees:

Go therefore on the wings of an eagle and search the mountains and valleys—scour the deserts and forests and sleep not until thou findest thrift and frugality! Take into thy soul these and know them! Give these knighted virtues prominence at the round table of thy kingdom, Thrift on thy left and Frugality on thy right, and thee and thine shall never know want again.

Notes

1. "Quotation by Daniel Defoe," http://www.quoteblock.com/quote/all-the-good-things-of-the-world-are-no-further/.
2. "Chapter 11," *Teachings of the Presidents of the Church: Spencer W. Kimball* (Salt Lake City: Intellectual Reserve, 2006), 115–23.
3. Brigham Young, *Discourses of Brigham Young* (Salt Lake City: Deseret Book, 1978), 213.
4. Brigham Young, *Discourses of Brigham Young*, vol. 8 (Salt Lake City: Deseret Book, 1978), 68.

"It is easier to collect money than to spend it wisely." —Luther Hodges[1]

Amazing Treasure Number Eleven

Saving: Middleclass Key to Wealth

Contrary to popular thought, the key to middleclass wealth is not in winning lottery tickets. It is not necessarily about making more money or even about making a lot of money. Some years ago, after watching me closely for several months a young married man asked me why I continued to bring sack lunches and take the bus to work every day. "You are completely debt free and still you act like a poor man," he exclaimed. "Think about what you just said," I replied. "A man who is out of debt still has no discretionary money! Although he is no longer a slave to others, he must now build a solid financial foundation by saving and wisely investing."

Unlike those who truly understand wealth accumulation, middle-class America reaches for a better life by spending money on unnecessary things. Daily we willingly surrender our monetary might to items we don't really need. To our detriment, we behave like children in a candy store in terms of buying things on credit. Yet when we borrow, we use hired soldiers and end up giving away many of our own for the privilege. By so doing we stay poor and make a few very rich.

The western United States has been growing so fast. Over the past century, planners have struggled to keep up with the challenges. To accomodate the ever-increasing demand for water, a group of strategists, engineers, and politicians designed and built a huge water bank, the Glen Canyon Dam near Page, Arizona. In order to hold in reserve a portion of the Colorado River, a huge and powerful wall with operating gates was erected between two steep canyon walls. One day at a time and one drop at a time, with the gates partially closed, the river would eventually fill the great reservoir with billions of gallons of water. Authorities estimated it would take forty years to fill to capacity.

Each one of us has a little financial stream meandering through our lives. I repeat, we need not be as concerned with the size of the stream as with the angle of the gates. As Cyril Nothcote Parkinson notes, unless we're clever, "expenditure always rises to meet income."[2] Isn't it interesting what you will not consider buying when you make $30,000 becomes pressing at $50,000 and indispensable at $80,000. Regardless of the size of your stream of income, you will have no accumulation unless you manually crank the gates partially closed. The excess will always flow downstream. In his book, *Standing For Something*, President Gordon B. Hinckley wrote:

> Dr James Clayton, professor of history and former dean of the graduate school at the University of Utah, has specialized, throughout his distinguished career, in the evaluation of economic history. He believes that public and private debt has become the most compelling international issue of our day. In December 1998, he explained his reasoning: "Back in the 1950s, 30 percent of [our] disposable income was debt. Now 92 percent of [our] disposable income is debt. The average American household has spent next year's entire income, and that is unprecedented in our history. Our savings rate is very, very low. A couple of weeks ago, it went below zero. That has not been true since the 1930s." He continued with a startling indictment, "Frugality is now a thing of the past, and deficit financing in the public sector and very high debt levels in the private sector [are routine]."[3]

Credit cards, automobiles, and thirty-year mortgages are middleclass America's Achilles heels when it comes to their inability to save.

Concerning his father, Lee Iaccoca wrote, "My father was a little ahead of his time. He foresaw that buying things on time and getting into hock would undermine people's sense of responsibility about money. He predicted that easy credit would eventually permeate and sabotage our entire society and that consumers would get into trouble by treating their little plastic cards as if they were money in the bank."[4]

We have a diehard rule in our home—absolutely no credit cards allowed. This has proven to be one of the wisest things we have ever done. Because we are human, we do not tempt ourselves with someone else's money. When credit card applications come in the mail, we simply shred them unopened. Credit cards complicate everything. By eliminating them, you train yourself to live within your paycheck. Therefore, treat credit cards as if they were toxic waste; get rid of them. Exceptionally few people have the discipline and accounting skills to properly use credit cards. (Credit cards will be discussed in more detail later in this book.)

Next, cancel as many monthly services as conceivably possible. Most of us do not need lawn services, cellular phones, additional phone services, cable or satellite television, newspaper and magazine subscriptions, gym memberships, or expensive internet services, especially while we are in debt. My younger brother once observed, "It's interesting everyone in the family has a cellular phone but you, and you're the only one among us who can afford one." If you haven't disciplined yourself to save for what you want, simply don't buy.

People are constantly making poor-man comments to me, such as, "You can afford to buy this, Jeff. This is chump change to you." Not too long ago, I was looking to buy a vacuum cleaner for our farm house. An overly zealous friend once advised that with my money I could afford to buy the very best vacuum, and he knew of an imported model for $1,500. He felt strongly I should buy it. Because he persisted, I explained, "I didn't get where I'm at buying $1,500 vacuum cleaners, and I wouldn't be there long if I started now." Several weeks later I spotted a practically new Kirby vacuum cleaner at a thrift store for $20.00.

Do the math. How many soldiers did I keep fighting on my side by exercising prudence, patience, and restraint? Of this I am certain, the day I adopt the "chump change" mindset will be the day my good fortune changes to bad. It won't make any difference how much money I make! I will eventually be poor.

During the season of building your sound financial foundation, do not fall into the trap of buying or leasing a new car. If you can get by with one car or a less expensive car or even no car at all, jump at the chance. You will free up a lot of money you can put to better use. And never call an automobile—new or old—an "investment." It's a money pit. Almost nothing loses value faster than a new car.

If I am a mouse and enjoy cheese, the most disastrous thing I can do is mess with cheese on a loaded trap. Conversely, if I'm a human trying to get out of debt, and enjoy a pension for new cars, the most irresponsible thing I could do is walk around a new car dealership tempting myself with the forbidden. Trust me, I know. Years ago a girl I was interested in was also dating another guy and he owned a fancy black sports car. It was much flashier than the simple, plain compact sedan I drove, and I ignorantly felt the need to compete. Therefore, I stopped off at a dealership to just sneak a peek at a car that caught my eye. The next thing I knew a clever salesman had lured me inside the dealership and began working his magic on me.

In a near hypnotic state, I reached over to sign loan papers when all at once I caught myself, stood up, and said, "No, I don't want to buy this car."

"You can't back out now," he warned. I apologized and thanked him for his time and began walking out. "What are you doing?" he yelled in an obvious attempt to shame me back into submission, "You're breaking all the rules."

"You really wouldn't sell a car to someone who can't afford it, would you?" I replied.

He continued, "But what will your neighbors and friends think when you pull up in this bad boy? Just imagine it," he said as he dangled the keys.

"Oh, they'd probably hate me for it," I replied as I continued out the door.

"But kid, what about the girl you're trying to impress," he said out of desperation. "She will probably pick the fancier ride."

"Then she's not worth having," I replied as the door shut behind me.

Wow! What a close call—a mistake that could have haunted me for years. I was no match for this clever salesman. In a relative short period of time, the salesman had discovered my emotional needs and weaknesses and skillfully exploited them. When I walked onto that dealership lot my intention wasn't to buy an expensive sports car, but that's what I almost did. I messed with the cheese on the loaded trap! Many salespersons believe if you step onto the lot, you'll drive home in one of their cars. It's that simple! They excel in both the science of overcoming objections and in the art of emotional selling. With the exception of picking up parts, I have only visited a dealership lot once since and that experience was similar to the first one.

And that's not the end of the story. My wife married the man of her dreams—me—remember, the guy in the plain car? Don't let anyone fool you. In the long run it won't matter much to your neighbors, family, or friends what you drive. Moreover, any girl or boy worth having searches the heart of the individual behind the wheel, and not the wheel itself. Years ago, my father told my older brother that his older, less attractive car gave him a definite advantage over the boys with new and fancy cars. He said, "Any girl who accepts a second date with you, is interested in you and not your horseless carriage. The other boys cannot be so certain."

I readily concede driving an old car isn't the most exciting concept. But keep in mind that I am not asking you to do it indefinitely. You can acquire a newer car when your debts are paid, when you establish a firm financial foundation, and of course, when you have saved the money to pay for it outright. I personally saved a great deal of money by driving older cars. Instead of making loan payments, paying interest, and having expensive comprehensive insurance premiums, I used the extra money to pay off mortgages and acquire investments.

But the process doesn't have to be drudgery. It can be as fun as you make it. My friend and I had a contest to see which of us could squeeze out the most miles from our cars. Both of our cars had over 150,000 miles on the odometer. Soon our office associates joined in the fun and made a big deal over the duel between my Dodge Colt and my friend's Volkswagen Rabbit. Our rules prohibited us from replacing the internal workings of the engine or transmission. Duct tape, bailing wire, or anything else was fair game. Friendly bets were wagered. The loser would buy dinner at the McDonalds in nearby Park City, Utah. Toward the end of the contest, my friend enlisted the help of two German mechanics by appealing to their national pride. For a couple of years they worked magic on the fledging Rabbit and managed to get it to pass the county's stringent emission control standards. But in the end, the Colt continued rolling! We both had a great time and milked every possible mile from our cars.

A national radio talk show host recently told a listener the answer to her boredom wasn't medication but the acquisition of an older car. I immediately began to laugh because I knew the truthfulness of his advice. I contemplated my own encounters with such vehicles of vintage character. There was the yellow 1982 Ford Fairmont station wagon my little family owned for many years. On one particular evening we were driving down Third Avenue in Salt Lake City, Utah, when Karl Malone of the Utah Jazz and his family pulled up next to us at an intersection in a custom Chevy Suburban. Excited, I announced the presence of the celebrity to my children, who where then stretching and straining to catch a peek. The Malone mobile was so bright and shiny I instantly became aware of my old, seriously outdated station wagon. To make things painfully worse, the sun was setting in the west, which highlighted the Fairmont's dirty front window shield. Before I could stop and weigh the full consequences of my actions, I hit the automatic windshield washer. In so doing I set into motion something I could not retract. You see, the passenger side jet nozzle was maladjusted and, when activated, would squirt a powerful several second stream of window cleaner in, you guessed it, Karl Malone's general direction.

As long as I wander upon this planet, there will remain permanently seared into my memory the bright blue fluid dripping from the front hood of Karl Malone's fancy ride, accompanied by the utter shock and disbelief expressed on the Malones' faces. Just when the moment couldn't get any tenser for me and my poor wife, Karl broke out in a laugh and then, taking the part of a gentleman proceeded to wave and dote over my children who had been staring at him. Duplicate that type of adventure in a late model Honda or Toyota. Some time after we left our mark on the Malone's suburban, my wife accidentally nailed her blue-blooded visiting teaching partner in the head with windshield wiper fluid and ruined her fancy new hairdo. Just between you and me, to this day I wonder if it was truly an accident.

Late one night as I was traveling to our little farm in Bear River Valley, I was listening to a national radio personality doling out financial advice to his listeners. One caller asked for advice on the type of car he and his wife should purchase. They wanted something that would turn heads, a car in the $60,000-plus range. He and his wife were young working professionals with a combined income of $160,000. They had saved $225,000 in the bank. The commentator listened carefully and asked probing questions about the couple's debt-to-income ratio. Finally, he instructed the listener that he would be better off driving the old vehicles he already owned and carefully investing the savings. The caller was offended and stubbornly resisted the advice. He felt their income and status warranted a new luxury car. But the commentator persisted, "At your age and with your modest savings, you have no business considering a depreciable expenditure of this magnitude. If your situation allows it, take the bus." I was so impressed by that advice that I spontaneously erupted into a cheer.

I have a theory if an individual were to personally sacrifice and save $40,000, he would never spend it on something that depreciates ten to twenty percent the minute it is driven off the dealer's lot and loses most of the rest of its value within five years. How can we call this an investment? Unfortunately, we don't focus on these facts because we use easily borrowed money, and the resulting price in interest, depreciation, taxes, insurance, and maintenance is astronomical. Returning to the metaphor of pennies as soldiers—buying a new car will cost you millions of lost troops. What kind of general would lead his valuable men into such a losing venture as this? This type of thinking will constantly keep the wage earner in the poorhouse.

For the vast majority of Americans, the single largest expense is their house. Even a modest mortgage puts a thirty-year stranglehold on family finances. I recently learned about two immigrant Asian boys who came to the United States in search of work and a better life. In three years, these boys worked odd jobs that paid only minimum wage. They saved enough money to completely pay for a home in Sandy, Utah. They also saved enough to bring their families to Utah from halfway around the world. When a local television station interviewed them, the two were asked how they accomplished such a task in adverse economic times. One of the boys responded, "We have never had so much work and been paid so well." He added, "This a great land of opportunity."

It is clear how unremarkable these boys understood their accomplishment to be. In three years they accomplished what takes many Americans thirty years. They only worked odd jobs, in a strange land where they could barely speak the language.

These young boys were not fettered by the long list of luxuries Americans have come to expect. In their native country, they were accustomed to living on the bare essentials. They could and did go without nice automobiles, expensive clothes, boats, and campers. They put off the purchase of fine furnishings for a few seasons. The big-screen television, stereo, and matching appliances were foreign to them and completely unnecessary. Frequently eating out at fancy restaurants and buying pricey prepared foods at grocery stores didn't make their list of necessities. Last but not least, they were not competing with the neighbors. William Wordsworth said, "The world is too much with us; late and soon,/ Getting and spending, we lay waste our powers."[5]

My grandmother would have been so impressed with these young men. They closed the gates to their financial dam so effectively that they were able to accumulate enough for a home in a short period of time. Can you imagine the relief? Can you imagine the newfound freedom? They will never have a mortgage payment.

What if our children were taught to satisfy their mortgages in just a few short years instead of thirty? Instead of being weeks or months away from homelessness, over their heads in debt, and splitting pennies to pay bills, our children could better enjoy their lives.

We would do well to learn more than the art of frugality from these boys. Americans have unwittingly overpriced themselves in the new and growing world market. The American labor force is among the highest paid in the world. Other countries are now producing similar products for much less cost. Because their products sell for less, they move off retail shelves faster and in greater numbers than their American counterparts. How long can we expect to keep this country's factories churning out products that are more expensive than foreign-made products? Many of us can see the writing on the wall and yet we are unwilling to make a single solitary concession. Through organized unions we choke the remaining life from American corporations by demanding higher wages and better benefits. Can we afford to turn a blind eye as we sit perched in our expensive homes and refuse to reduce our lifestyle or alter our strategy? We must wake up and face the facts that the international economic dynamics have changed, and the rules for saving and financial stability have been rewritten to favor the lean and less encumbered.

These two boys clearly demonstrated they could walk all over us fat cats and do it in our own country. I wonder if we could do the same in theirs. Let us be wise and learn from them. If we don't do it voluntarily now, we will be forced in the future.

Again, it is important to break down the larger intimidating goals to smaller, more manageable ones. If your goal is to pay your house off in ten years, be sure to celebrate each year you meet this goal. Each celebration should be better than the last. People around you will begin to wonder why you're always so cheerful.

Recently I heard a middle-aged man, who enjoyed a well paying job, boast he had declared bankruptcy three times in his life. This man is part of a growing, worrisome trend of deteriorating personal responsibility. The current national mortgage crisis was brought upon us by wide-scale greed and overindulgence. Bankruptcies rose 57 percent from the first quarter of 2007 to the first quarter of 2008. One of the main purposes behind bankruptcy laws is to provide some relief for financial disasters, which are largely beyond a company or individual's control—not as a net to protect people from their greed and financial recklessness.

If we utilize bankruptcy in this manner, we take from others what isn't ours. Years ago I put a down payment on a home which went into bankruptcy courts before the sale was complete. At some point, during the year-long process, we received a document regarding the many trusting people and businesses that had provided products or services to the declaree, along with the corresponding amount they were left holding. Many were owed tens of thousands of dollars—the total amount was in the hundreds of thousands. Much of the debt included extravagances and luxuries such as fancy automobiles, barns, horse trailers, camping trailers, and decorative fencing. Many of the assets in question had been put in the mother's name, apparently in anticipation of bankruptcy. This makes it difficult if not impossible for courts to go after them. I was also informed this was not the first time this party had declared bankruptcy. Unfortunately, there are loopholes that make pursuing such a course legal, but the action is morally wrong and God will one day hold us accountable. In the words of Thomas Carlyle, "Great is bankruptcy: the great bottomless gulf into which all falsehoods, public and private, do sink, disappearing."[6] My grandmother would turn in her grave to see such financial recklessness, waste, and dishonesty. Marvin J. Ashton warned,

> Please listen carefully to this—and if it makes some of you feel uncomfortable, it is on purpose: Latter-day Saints who ignore or avoid their creditors are entitled to feel the inner frustrations that such conduct merits, and they are not living as Latter-day Saints should! Bankruptcy should be avoided, except only under the most unique and irreversible circumstances, and then utilized only after prayerful thought and thorough legal and financial consultation.[7]

A university employee and young father related to me the time he bought sack lunches for a prominent church leader and his wife out of his own pocket because they had encountered some unexpected delays. A few days later he received a note of appreciation with enough money to more than cover the expenses. I imagine the prompt payment of this debt was a matter of honor to this couple. What if each of us approached our lives with this type of genuine concern for others? Wouldn't the vast majority of bankruptcies virtually dry up?

Furthermore, we salute those extraordinary individuals who through no fault of their own are left holding enormous debt and yet refuse to transfer it to the backs of others by declaring bankruptcy. Dime by dime, dollar-by-dollar, year after long year, they quietly pay back every single penny. I know there is a special place in heaven for people of such undaunting character.

In the overall process, we must never forget true wealth and monetary accumulation are byproducts of obedience to eternal laws—timeless principles such as honesty and thrift—not financial recklessness or overindulgences.

I would like to share with you another profound secret. Once you're on your way, saving money can be as contagious as spending it. When I was in my early teens one of our neighbors, Cal Smith, opened his wallet and showed me a very thick stack of one hundred dollar bills tucked inside. He then taught me, "Jeff, get into the habit of saving these bills, the first one thousand dollars is by far the most difficult. It gets much easier saving the second, third, fourth and so on."

I have put it to the test and discovered Brother Smith's advice to be amazingly accurate. Once we are clear and free from debt, we can begin to pay ourselves. I recommend a target of 10 to 20 percent savings from each paycheck that we strive to achieve, but if this is not attainable, don't panic; in the beginning 2 or 3 percent is better than nothing at all.

Merrill Lynch conducted a study showing nearly two out of three baby boomers weren't saving enough money to maintain current living standards when they retired. Even more alarming was the discovery that 40 percent of boomers saved less than a thousand dollars a year; 33 percent saved absolutely nothing. It should be noted Social Security survives by taxing current workers to support retirees. In 1950, it took sixteen workers to support one retiree. In contrast, by 2030, it is estimated there will be only two workers available to support each retiree. Additionally, Americans are living longer today than they were when Social Security was created. Life expectancy back then was sixty-two years old. Today it is well into the eighties.[8] Unless the federal government performs major surgery, Social Security is on a collision course with destiny. And it is not likely a seriously debt-weighted federal government can afford to bail it out. Therefore, if your employer offers matching funds for a tax-deferred retirement plan or a 401k retirement plan, enroll in it—now!

Of course, fewer and fewer companies are offering to pay retirees a percentage of their salary. "Defined benefit" plans are rapidly being replaced by "defined contribution" plans, wherein the responsibility is shifting from the employer to the employee. Defined contribution plans require employees to contribute a percentage of pre-tax income to generate a retirement fund. For this reason, it is imperative we plan for our future by setting up some type of retirement fund and religiously contributing to it with every paycheck.

Although it is never too late to plan for your future, begin contributing to your retirement fund as early in your career as possible. The interest and matching funds will have a longer period to compound. Time harnessed properly has a tremendous earning potential. Compare the following two strategies:

Early saver, Susan, saves $1,000 a year for ten years at 8 percent interest compounded daily. Then she stops, having saved a total of $10,000. She leaves her stash alone to build. Late saver, Bill, doesn't darken a bank door for a decade. In the eleventh year, he gets religion and starts saving $1,000 a year, also at 8 percent. Forty years later, he has saved $40,000. But he still hasn't caught up with Susan, and never will! He can go on depositing $1,000 a year until the millennium. At 8 percent interest, the Early Saver (although still depositing no more money) will pull further ahead of the Late Saver every year.[9]

As you can clearly see, the early sacrifice will greatly increase your future nest egg. If you put off saving today, you may never catch up to where you could have been. Interest on money you've saved works for you around the clock. Instead of paying interest on debt, you're receiving it, and the math works out to be nearly double the savings. A major secret to attaining wealth is to find ways to earn money in your absence. You can only work a limited number of hours in a day, but invested money works for you without your being there. Matching company funds and interest earned in 401k plans fits this criterion perfectly.

Spending less than you make is the great equalizer. It will make a poor man rich. After all, if you don't learn to live on less than you make, you will never have the opportunity to live on more than you make. Long ago, Confucius taught his students, "When prosperity comes, do not use all of it."[10]

Remember: the trick to this whole game is to override ego-driven impulses by making responsible decisions. Once we have reduced our lifestyle to the bare essentials, our greatest possibilities surface. Too many of us are poor because we practice the poor man's habits. How long can millionaires afford to live like billionaires? For that matter, how long can middle-class America afford to live like millionaires? Yet we desperately and futilely attempt to live a Dillard's, Nordstrom's, or Saks Fifth Avenue lifestyle on a thrift store income and we're forever frustrated because we're deep in debt and can't save a dime to save our lives. Said Sir Ernest Benn, "It is easy to make the rich poor, but it is not so easy, we have discovered, to make the poor rich."[11] Conversely, if you were willing to live like a church mouse for a strategic period of time, you would start the engine of a machine that would run for the rest of your life.

Do we want to be a part of what Daniel describes as the stone rolling forth as it consumes the world? Or will we be stranded on the sidelines, buried in debt? The ancient prophets looked upon our day and time with anticipation and wonder. In the grand scheme of things, it is to be the time of all times! But I ask you, how can we shoulder more responsibilities in our wards and stakes; how can we reach out to help and uplift the poor and fatherless if we're shackled in chains? How can we serve multiple missions if we're strapped to two or three jobs trying to pay for it all? Spiritually speaking, how can we hear the still small voice with such a loud and obnoxious preoccupation? Is the great and wondrous caravan passing us by? Our core beliefs suggest that men are that they might have joy, not misery.

Like the immense pull of the moon on earth's massive oceans, the eleventh amazing treasure possesses the power to shift financial misfortune into peace and prosperity. The treasure states:

With a simple reduction of accustomed things, a serious sheering of wants and even a reduction of high-end needs, creates a combustible environment for savings. Hence, from this day forward spend less than you make, wisely invest the difference and save, save, save! "If you wish to get rich, save what you get. A fool can earn money; but it takes a wise man to save and dispose of it to his own advantage."[12]

Contrary to anything else you might have been taught, this is the secret key to unlocking middle-class wealth.

Notes

1. Luther Hodges in *Richard Evans' Quote Book* (Salt Lake City: Publishers Press, 1971) 228.
2. Cyril Northcote Parkinson in *Richard Evans' Quote Book* (Salt Lake City: Publishers Press, 1971) 229.
3. Gordon B. Hinckley, *Standing for Something* (New York: Random House, 2000), 85.
4. Lee Iacocca with William Novak, *Iacocca: An Autobiography* (New York:

Bantam, 1984), 9.

5. William Wordsworth, "The World Is Too Much With Us; Late and Soon," http://www.online-literature.com/wordsworth/546/.
6. Thomas Carlyle, *The French Revolution: A History*, vol. 10 (New York: Peter Fenlon Collier, 1897), 64.
7. Marvin J. Ashton, "Guide to Family Finance," *Liahona*, Apr. 2000, (adapted from Apr. 1975 General Conference address).
8. "Babyboomers: Savings of 40-, 50-Year Olds Are Insufficient," Knight-Ridder New Service (Philadelphia).
9. Jane Bryant Quinn, *Making the Most of Your Money* (New York: Simon & Schuster, 1991).
10. Confucius, "Quotations about Prosperity," http://www.quotegarden.com/prosperity.html.
11. Sir Ernest Benn in *Richard Evans' Quote Book* (Salt Lake City: Publishers Press, 1971), 227.
12. Brigham Young, *Discourses of Brigham Young*, sel. John A. Widtsoe (Salt Lake City: Deseret Book Co., 1941), 292.

"Nothing in the world can take the place of persistence. Talent will not; nothing is more common than unsuccessful men with talent. Genius will not; unrewarded genius is almost a proverb. Education will not; the world is full of educated derelicts. Persistence and determination alone are omnipotent." —Calvin Coolidge[1]

Amazing Treasure Number Twelve

Determination: Tie a Knot and Hang On!

A few years ago I read a news article about a man who had been traveling through the northern mountains of California in the winter. Caught in a virtual whiteout, he had to park his truck and wait out the storm. The storm continued unabated and soon the man was stranded. Several days later, he was found dead in the cab of his truck. Tragically, only yards ahead of him the roads had been clear. Apparently he had never left his truck to scout out the area or find help. He had just remained in the truck and given up.

During World War II, Sir Winston Churchill became famous for his saying, "Never give in, never give in, *never, never, never, never.*"[2] Simple, yet so powerful! One by one, freedom-loving people heard the courageous voice of this incredible leader and followed the example of his unconquerable spirit. We can take a lesson from Churchill as we face our seemingly insurmountable foes. Dogged persistence and an unwavering determination to fight will cause our enemy to yield and eventually be conquered.

Sam Walton wrote, "When folks have asked me, 'How did Walmart do it?' . . . [I would answer,] friend, we just got after it and stayed after it."[3]

John D. Hess said, "Great men are said to have four things in common: . . . they speak softly, have the capacity for hard work, a deep conviction for their cause, and a consuming belief in their ability to do it."[4]

Your goal of becoming independent may seem overwhelming and impossible, but don't become discouraged! The ship of Captain John Paul Jones's was nearly decimated in a battle when the British officer asked if he wished to surrender. To his enemies' utter disbelief Captain Jones responded, "I have not yet begun to fight!"[5]

A wise man once said, "Mountains viewed from a distance seem to be unscalable; but they can be climbed; and the way to begin is to take the first upward step. From that moment the mountains are less high. The slopes that seem so steep from a distance seem to level off as we near them."[6] You will win this battle by fighting it from paycheck to paycheck, from day to day, and from penny to penny. You will encounter clever opponents who will be anxious to take your precious dollars away from you, but don't give in. Again, "no" is a powerful word.

The Salt Lake Temple was forty years in the making and was constructed almost entirely by the hand labor of an impoverished people. It has now become symbolic of the restored gospel and the indefatigable LDS people. With little more than crude tools and beasts of burden, through sacrifice, dedication, and raw ingenuity, they created one of the most beautiful and inspiring edifices on earth. Many who worked on it would never see its completion. Faced with nearly insurmountable obstacles, they carved thousands of stones from a distant quarry and transported them the long distance to Salt Lake City. Here at the construction site, each piece was meticulously cut to size and laid into place. Many times I have visited this temple, walked around its sacred grounds, and taken inspiration from the sacrifice and determination of those pioneers. Each time I have come away with the confident reassurance that I can do anything I set my mind and heart upon.

Determination is the act or habit of deciding definitely and firmly; persistence is sticking with something longer than the obstacle has the will to resist. Just look at what the small Colorado River did to the Grand Canyon. Little by little, it carved out a huge gorge and turned it into one of the wonders of the world! "The greatest results in life are usually attained by simple means and the exercise of ordinary qualities. These may for the most part be summed in these two—common sense and perseverance."[7]

One day I came across an ad for feeder calves. I was in the process of populating my little farm with animals, so I went to have a look. The farmer had several to choose from, but he practically twisted my arm and offered a discount if I would buy one particular cow. The price was too good to pass up. However, I should have seen a red flag when the farmer delivered the cow several days early. I should have seen another red flag when he looked over my property and muttered, "It's a good thing you've got a sturdy fence living next to that busy road."

Early the next morning I awakened to the sound of honking horns and screeching tires. It took me half a day to get the cow rounded up and back into the pasture. Soon after, I received a call that the cow was blocking traffic at Riverton, Utah's main intersection. Thereafter, it became a common sight to see us chasing the cow up and down the road or dragging it back to the pasture with our truck. Our phone never stopped ringing

By now our expensive milled fence was in shambles, and it was becoming increasingly more difficult to keep the cow corralled. I was nearing the stage of developing an uncontrollable facial twitch due to a poorly bred cow.

One day I noticed the cow grazing in a neighboring pasture. Why she had broken through two fences to get in that pasture I'll never understand. The grass was thicker and greener in *her* pasture. No matter how much I fought back the enveloping fog of insanity, I snapped! I dropped what I was doing and began recklessly chasing the cow all over the two-acre field trying to get a rope around her neck.

I ran so long and so hard I eventually fell to the ground exhausted, unable to take another step. With growing concerns, two good-hearted neighbors came to my rescue. One was a real cowboy. Under his instruction, we corralled the cow in a corner and the cowboy, in beautiful rodeo fashion, threw his lasso over the cow's head. Lurching forward, the cow bellowed and bolted for freedom.

She trampled over me, pulling the cowboy behind—now in haste and without his hat. She was moving so fast the cowboy had to let go of the rope. She broke through a barbed wire fence on a dead run and soon disappeared into a large field, rope and all. The dust hadn't yet settled when I sold the cow—at a loss—to the cowboy. Still laughing, he jumped into his truck and sped off to saddle up his roping horse.

Did I mention something inside me snapped? My story should have ended here, but instead I walked to the broken fence and spotted the cow in a far corner of the pasture. A thought transfixed me, "You miserable, over-stuffed, rotting leather carcass, I have a score to settle with you!"

The cow was so winded I was able to walk within fifty feet of her. She eyed me with distrust. Never before had I felt so unattached to those virtues that distinguish humans from mere animals. My sanity narrowed to a dangerous level and I found myself giving in further. Leopard-like I rushed her, pounced on the rope, and quickly wrapped it around my glove several times. Not until the startled cow hurdled over me with the ease of an Olympian did it hit me like a sledgehammer—this hadn't been one of my best ideas. Before I could reconsider, the rope went taut, my head whipped back, and my arms nearly ripped from their sockets. The next thing I knew I was being pulled through a wet and muddy field at breakneck speed. Despite being dragged over rocks, bushes, stickers, mud, and manure, I wouldn't let go. Even to prolong the life of my children's father, I wouldn't let go. Round and round the pasture we went until the cow finally collapsed. Sore and covered with mud, I struggled over and tied the rope around the cow's legs and then collapsed next to my prisoner. In my mind, I was the clear winner! We remained in our respective positions until the cowboy arrived on his horse.

To this day I don't think the cowboy understood why this city boy in a white shirt and slacks was sitting in the mud next to his newly purchased cow. Intrigued, he circled us a few times, shook his head, and said, "What on earth are you doing with my cow, Red?"

Wiping mud from my chin and out of my eyes, I tried to sound intelligent. "Just grabbed the devil by the tail and hung on for all I was worth."

Whittling away at debt and exercising financial self-control is at times like being dragged by a runaway cow. The rocks and the stickers are painful. The mud and manure are humiliating. But letting go means surrendering. Franklin Roosevelt put it this way: "When you get to the end of your rope, tie a knot and hang on."[8]

Anytime we move toward righteousness or self-empowerment, Satan will try to discourage or prevent it. It is so predictable you can set your clock to it. An inspired bishop can expect more opposition than an uncommitted member, who occasionally sticks his foot into the ring. Joseph Smith, a young, poor, and insignificant farm boy, was slated to become the Lord's mouthpiece and open the last dispensation of the fulness of times, and though others were ignorant of his role, Satan certainly was not! He was thoroughly acquainted with this young boy from the eternities and clearly understood he had a pivotal mission to perform on earth. Is it any wonder he was waiting for Joseph in the grove of trees? Is it a surprise he attacked him before he could even begin his prayer? With no veil to shroud his memory, Satan knew the signs; he knew Joseph would prove to be a great disturber to his undisputed reign over centuries of darkness.

Although Joseph was delivered from the ambush in the grove by the visitation of God the Father and His Son Jesus Christ, Satan would prove tenacious and unrelenting. From that moment to Carthage, he was determined to never let Joseph enjoy another moment of peace. He tormented him at every turn and at every climb. With the advent of the First Vision, Satan's days were numbered, and with weeping, wailing, and gnashing of teeth, the master of hate and deception threw everything he could at the young boy.

While we may not be engaged in something as important as restoring the gospel, each of us can make a difference if we so choose. If you're positively altering the direction of your life, or assisting others to do the same, brace yourself for some turbulence.

I had been very sick for several months, and the doctors were uncertain what was wrong. Through my wife's countless efforts, and after several long months, I began to see signs of improvement. On one particular Sunday, she encouraged me to accompany her and the children to church. I hadn't been for months, and she felt the change would do me good. I needed more time and resisted. But after the family left, I continued thinking about it and at some point decided to get dressed and go. After the rigors of showering and dressing, I was so utterly worn out I nearly gave up the notion. Instead, I put one foot in front of the other, walked out the door, and down the street. As I passed by a neighbor's house, two coonhounds lying on the front lawn and soaking in the mountain valley sun, suddenly decided I looked like breakfast. As if possessed, they charged me with gnashing teeth. Too weak to run, I turned to meet my attackers. Thanks to my years of training and the miracle of adrenaline, I gave the large male a hard snap-kick to the lower jaw. Yelping and shaking his head, he backed away a few yards. Coming fast to his rescue, the smaller female was aggressively seeking to bite my leg when she was met with a hard blow about the nose from the back of my fist. Startled and crouching, she held her ground and continued after my leg. Regrouped and even madder than before, the male charged again, this time from the other side. Just about the time I was ready to collapse from dizziness and exhaustion, a loud commanding voice sounded from the yard that sent the dogs retreating—tails between legs—back to the front yard. It was the owner! "I don't know what got into those dogs," he said, as he apologized and asked me if I was going to be okay. I did my best to remain standing and reassured my neighbor I would be fine after a few minutes. My first response was to give up, go back home, and retire to bed where I belonged. Instead, I dug deep inside for strength, said a little prayer, and continued forward. I don't know how many times I had walked by that house without so much as a bark from those dogs. It was one of the strangest things I ever witnessed.

This day would prove to be a pivotal turning point in recovering from my illness. I needed the association and healing spirit of church attendance. Inscribe it in stone: anytime you have snapping dogs at your feet, smile, duck your head, and plow forward with courage. It's a sure sign you're doing something right and worthwhile! As a matter of fact, if aggressive dogs aren't present in your life, perhaps you should fall to your knees and ask the Lord why. And, if by chance you've been a snapping dog to someone, stay on those knees and beg the Lord's forgiveness, and then get up and straightforwardly seek forgiveness from the injured party.

For in the minefields of eternal wealth, we will one day discover that the realization of our dreams is intertwined with helping others realize theirs. Unfortunately, we have not collectively arrived at this understanding. Therefore, heed the advice Edgar Degas gave to the struggling ballerina, Marie, "Everyone has what it takes to fail; to succeed is a far harder thing. . . . Everyone in this life will try and take your dreams away from you, only you can see them through; you're on your own with them. You have to hold them tightly in your heart even when giving up would be the easiest thing to do."[9]

The twelfth amazing treasure can crumble barriers, move mountains and significantly empower its benefactor. The treasure holds:

Impossiblities are made possible when the body's billions of microscopic cells are ignited and ablaze with a common cause. "The secret of success is the constancy of purpose."[10] Therefore, "Fight one more round. When your arms are so tired that you can hardly lift your hands to come on guard, fight one more round. When your nose is bleeding and your eyes are black and you are so tired that you wish your opponent would crack you one on the jaw and put you to sleep, fight one more round—remembering that the man who always fights one more round is never whipped."[11]

Notes

1. "Quotes by Calvin Coolidge," http://findquotes.com/quote/by/Calvin_Coolidge.
2. Winston Churchill, *Never Give In! The Best of Winston Churchill's Speeches*,(New York: Hyperion, 2003), 307.
3. Sam Walton, *Sam Walton, Made in America* (New York: Doubleday, 1992).
4. John D. Hess in *Richard Evans' Quote Book* (Salt Lake City: Publishers Press, 1971), 57.
5. John Paul Jones in *The New Dictionary of Cultural Literacy*, 3rd ed., edited by E. D. Hirsch, Jr. et. al. (Boston: Houghton Mifflin, 2002).
6. Anonymous, "Quotes about Mountains," http://www.myfavoriteezines.com/ezinedirectory/quotes-about-mountains.html.
7. Owen Feltham in *Richard Evans' Quote Book* (Salt Lake City: Publishers Press, 1971), 38.
8. "Memorable Quotes and quotations from Franklin D. Roosevelt," http://www.memorable-quotes.com/Franklin+d+roosevelt,a646.html.
9. *Degas and the Dancer*, VHS, directed by Ian D. Clark (1998, New Media Resources Video, 1999).
10. "Quote from Benjamin Disraeli," http://www.quoteworld.org/quotes/11322.
11. James Corbett in "Determination Keeps You Moving Til the Victory Comes," Mike Sigers, Oct. 31, 2007, http://www.simplenomics.com/determination-keeps-you-moving-til-the-victory-comes/.

"Seek ye diligently and teach one another words of wisdom; yea, seek ye out of the best books words of wisdom; seek learning, even by study, and also by faith." D&C 88:118

"If any of you lack wisdom, let him ask of God, that giveth to all men liberally, and upbraideth not; and it shall be given him." James 1:5

Amazing Treasure Number Thirteen

Sound Decisions: The Polar Star of Wealth

Almost effortlessly a life's savings can be completely decimated in a moment of foolishness, haste, or greed. I have seen it one too many times. Suffice it to say there is a reason why Utah is known as the capital of scam artists. They come here because we are easy pickings. Unfortunately, our religious and believing culture is only one head of this ugly twin. The other is often greed.

If *want* is the devil in fine print, then *greed* is his home. If we are not constantly guarding ourselves against greed, we can become its prey. Greed can motivate rational people to jump into unwise investments or business ventures way out of their league. I am aware of too many individuals who jumped headfirst into financial ruin.

Perhaps one of the greatest lessons I've learned while working near the Church's inner circle is its effective use of councils—groups of people from all walks of life who come together for a common goal or cause. The Church's effective mode of governance is the envy of religions, corporations, and world governments.

From top to bottom, councils and committees govern the Church. When decisions are made at any level in the Church, councils of fine people pray and deliberate over the important issues.

The scriptures teach us there are councils in heaven. "According to that which was ordained in the midst of the Council of the Eternal God of all other gods before this world was, that should be reserved unto the finishing and end thereof, when every man shall enter into his eternal presence and into his immortal rest" (D&C 121:32). "And the Gods took counsel among themselves and said: Let us go down and form man in our image, after our likeness; and we will give him dominion over the fish of the sea, and over the fowl of the air, and over the cattle, and over all the earth, and over every creeping thing that creepeth upon the earth" (Abraham 4:26).

One day a friend approached me concerning a business venture he was considering. He and a few associates wanted to start a limousine transportation service. To raise the necessary capital, each partner mortgaged his home for $65,000 and placed it into a general business account. Red flag number one! Never use the equity of your family's dwelling for speculative endeavors. Consider it sacred money.

He then mentioned the president of the company was a complete stranger. Red flag number two. Never trust large amounts of money to an unknown person, even if he makes claims of high returns.

Deftly, the president talked the talk and threw a little money around, and soon the local boys swallowed the act hook, line, and sinker. They believed this fast-talking stranger over family and friends, who advised greater caution. Whenever the local investors questioned him, he would counter with comments like, "Don't listen to the crabs, they're just trying to pull you back in the bucket . . . You can trust me. My wife is an inactive member of your church."

In a few short weeks he convinced my associates to follow him, promising them wealth. It was as though a venomous snake had bitten them. They had completely lost the power of reason. Soon they began to talk extravagantly about the many ways they would spend their money. Greed's insidious allure gripped them in an unbreakable trance. In Proverbs 16:18 we read, "Pride goeth before destruction." Their moment of glory ended with a painful crash. The stranger eventually skipped town, and the money disappeared with him.

Though the outcome may appear incredibly obvious to you, be extremely wary of likable, smooth talking strangers who promise the world and ask for your money. Again, when you consider any big financial decisions, seek the advice of wise loved ones, friends, and professionals.

If you are determined to start a business venture, you should remember 20 percent of Utah's bankruptcies in 2002 were credited to failed, start-up businesses. Notwithstanding, if you have dogged determination and have carefully thought it through, I recommend you choose a business in your field of expertise. This precaution will save you a great deal of grief as well as your financial future. Moonlighting is the safest way to break into the business world. Moonlighting assures that your financial bases are covered, and it allows you to grow and operate the business before jumping in full time.

Moonlighting provides a window of opportunity to test interest, resolve, and ability before placing significant personal investment on the line. If the elements of success exist, these ventures can be nurtured into legitimate businesses. During this developmental time, you can learn the trade secrets and the vital do's and don'ts that can be the kiss of death in the world of business. If you happen to fail, your investment will be small. The trick is to protect yourself from as much financial risk as possible while following your dream.

Despite the most thorough planning, your best-laid plans can go awry even when you go about them the right way. Just the announcement of a new Walmart or Home Depot coming to town can break the backs of nearby, small businesses. Entrepreneurs must accept the many risks and protect themselves as much as possible. These types of unknown variables are difficult if not impossible to plan for.

I am an entrepreneur at heart. I have tried my hand at a couple of low-profile businesses. I have learned that, contrary to public perception, a business owner's life is not his own. Some are cut out for it, but many are not. The demands upon your time and pocketbook are grueling and relentless. I have come to prefer part ownership of others' business ventures through the acquisition of highly diversified mutual funds, index funds, and stock holdings. By doing so, I partake of the companies' successes or failures, but I do not need to run the companies myself.

A few years ago tech-stocks defied both logic and gravity. The skyrocketing assent was unprecedented. This phenomenon brought out the worst in many investors. People borrowed and leveraged to buy more and more tech-stocks. One of my associates crunched some numbers on a high-risk, once-in-a-lifetime stock, and decided he could make millions if he borrowed and invested the money. The figures were so compelling that he went forward with his high-risk venture. The stock he bought was hot and it seemed as though its speedy ascent would never taper off. Even I, Mr. Conservative, found myself looking on with envy. If the stock continued to climb at its current rate, my associate would soon be rich. Everything was going so well that he bought more by maxing out several credit cards. I was astounded at his willingness to risk all he owned and his entire financial future on the performance of this one single stock.

Although he was breaking every rule in the book, it appeared he was getting away with it. The excitement was consuming, and soon other people followed suit. If his high-stake gamble paid off, he would make millions; if it failed he would spend the rest of his life paying it back. Today, the dust has settled and my associate walks around like a zombie. His venture failed and greed claimed one more casualty. It is exceedingly difficult, if not impossible, to recover from such a setback. Remember if it sounds too good to be true, it probably is. It would, therefore, be well to never invest borrowed money or money you can't afford to lose—like the equity of your family's home. And when you do invest, don't forget the two cardinal rules: diversify and seek out wise council.

Be wary of unsubstantiated stories, no matter how faith promoting. When I was working with one of our latter-day leaders, a member of my ward tapped me on the shoulder and requested to speak with me privately. When we found a private corner, he quietly stated that one of his friend's relatives knew somebody who had had a one-on-one meeting with this leader. This person had some money to invest and had mentioned this to my friend, the prominent leader. Supposedly, the leader's response was, "Buy food storage." The man explained that he already had his food storage. He wanted instead to invest some of his discretionary money that he had saved. Again, the leader was supposed to have said, "Buy food storage." Presumably, the scenario played out three times before the leader sternly warned, "Buy food storage because in a few months you won't be able to buy food." This was during the time that the United States had just sent missiles to Libya and the possibility of war was growing.

After my friend heard of "the meeting," he quickly borrowed a large sum of money and did as the leader had supposedly instructed. He purchased food storage. I knew that this leader had never met with this fictitious "somebody," and I tried to warn my friend. He became disillusioned and angry with me. He said I didn't know what I was talking about. He ended up with enormous debt and food storage in every closet. The predicted time of the disaster came and went and the tragedies never happened.

We must use sound judgment in our decisions and not take counsel from our fears or greediness. If this individual had really thought about his decision and sought the advice of wise people, he might have reached the conclusion that the story was just a story—and a bad one. Accepting every faith-promoting rumor that comes along can be very dangerous. There is a well-established chain of command set up by the Lord that is never circumvented. Do you want your temporal and spiritual salvation to come off the street or from the mouth of the prophet? We can rest assured that when the Lord has a specific message to give us He will do so as quickly as possible through proper channels.

I wish to share with you an ancient parable:

Once in a far away land there lived a wealthy landlord who called three of his servants together to reward them for years of loyal service. The lord took his servants to the high castle tower and said unto them, as he waved his hand across the distant country, "My land extends as far as the eye can see in every direction. I would that each of you have a portion of my land for your own families." The wise and wealthy lord instructed them that he would give them as much land as they could encircle in one day. The next morning he gave them a day's ration of food and water and bid them farewell. As the three servants departed, the Lord cautioned them to only take as much land as they needed. He also warned them to return before the sun went down in the western desert or they would no longer qualify. And so off they went.

Greed overtook the first servant, as he went too far and didn't calculate when to turn for home. He was desirous to take as much land as he could possibly get for he was strong and fit and could run miles without tiring. He was certain he would be the wealthiest of the servants. Secretly, he wanted more land than his master had. He ran farther and farther from the castle, which eventually became a distant dot on the horizon. Soon he could no longer see it. Still he ran on, and as he ran he wanted more and more. Before he realized it the shadows of night had befallen him.

The second servant started out more slowly and methodically. "I must pace myself," he thought, "for I must be careful to return seconds before nightfall." He was desirous to have as much property as time allowed. He wasn't as strong as the first, and so he carefully planned his strategy. But as he walked, he decided to walk just a little farther than his plan allowed. If only he could get to that beautiful spring, he thought, then he would quickly return. But as the sun's shadow speedily fell upon him, his strength failed him. When he had almost made the full circle, he dropped to the ground exhausted unable to take another step.

The third servant, not wanting to take advantage of his lord, only stepped off that which he needed and returned long before evening. The lord, overseeing the acts of his three servants, said to the third, "You have shown gratitude and wisdom in your choices. Today, I make you steward over all my lands."

When we encounter financial trouble in our lives, we have often chosen as the two greedy servants. Consequently, if we are to be happy, we need to choose as did the wise and thankful servant. If "sufficient for our needs" will not satisfy us, we will never be happy, and we will become vulnerable to greed's grip. Our Lord has given us this guidance, "Seek not for riches but for wisdom, and behold, the mysteries of God shall be unfolded unto you, and then shall you be made rich. Behold, he that hath eternal life is rich" (D&C 6:7).

Sound judgment is often the only thing that separates the rich from the poor and the happy from the miserable. Therefore we must effectively seek after the advice from the wise among us. Remember, if it looks too good to be true, it probably is.

Few things in my life have yielded more bang for the buck than the councils I have formed to help me make important decisions. These councils have prevented me from making emotional and foolish decisions that would have caused my family pain. Seeking wise advice is key to achieving sound judgment. With all the facts and thoughts before us, we stand the greatest chance of making the best possible decisions.

Wherefore, with wisdom gleaned from ages past the thirteenth amazing treasure boldly decrees:

Wisdom is not found in the valleys amidst the common or crowd; but unto a few who dance atop snowcapped peaks and from God who bestowed it upon them. Notwithstanding, the fount of wisdom is ever flowing from heaven's gate and can quench thirst best on bended knee. Moreover, "Each good man has in himself a quiet place wherein he lives however torn seemingly by the passions of the world. That is his citadel, which must be kept inviolate against assaults. That quiet place must be founded upon a rock and the rock must be a belief, a fervent and passionate belief, in the existence of the ultimate good, and a [decision] to put forth his strength against the ultimate evil."[1]

Wisdom as this have few men.

Notes

1. Dr. Foster Kennedy in *Richard Evans' Quote Book* (Salt Lake City: Publishers Press, 1971), 208.

"You see things; and you say why? But I dream things that never were; and I say why not?" —George Bernard Shaw[1]

Amazing Treasure Number Fourteen

The Mystical Mind: Its Invaluable Power of Creation!

At one stage of my life I was at the top of my game. For years I had proven myself and worked my way into a senior position of responsibility. During a yearly interview, my boss rated me so high it was literally off the charts. It appeared, at least in his eyes, I could do no wrong. As he wrapped up the verbal part of the interview, he said something that temporarily disappointed me. "Jeff," he said, "I expect even bigger things from you. If there is one thing that holds you back, it is that you have no idea what you're capable of accomplishing. You, my friend, underestimate your abilities. This year, I want you to dig deep and discover what it is I so clearly see in you."

As Jack London said, "[Wouldn't you] rather be ashes than dust! [Wouldn't you] rather that [your] spark burn out in a brilliant blaze than it should be stifled by dryrot. [Wouldn't you] rather be a superb meteor, every atom in magnificent glow, than a sleepy planet. The proper function of man is to live, not to exist. I shall not waste my days in trying to prolong them. I shall use my time."[2]

All things are made twice; first in the mind and next physically. This is an important eternal principle that God understands and employs. "For I, the Lord God, created all things, of which I have spoken, spiritually, before they were naturally upon the face of the earth" (Moses 3:5). In *The Sound of Music,* Maria touches on this profound principle in song: "Nothing comes from nothing, nothing ever could."[3] Therefore, if a dream is not properly programmed into the mind, it is not going to happen—nothing comes from nothing!

The human mind is the most amazing device ever known to man. Some scientists believe we only use 5 percent of the brain's total capability. Have you ever wondered how to employ the other 95 percent? For centuries, schools have expended enormous time and energy filling children's minds with facts and little time teaching children about the mind's great power and capability. Is it any wonder we use such a small portion of our brain's capacity?

The *Chicago Tribune* and Henry Ford had a high-profile, turbulent relationship. On one occasion the *Tribune* called Ford an ignoramus. Ford retaliated with some words of his own and demanded the *Tribune* prove its accusation. During the court proceedings, the attorneys for the *Tribune* grilled Ford about important historical events and dates. Because Ford hadn't received much formal education, he couldn't provide the answers. As the questioning continued, the humiliation mounted and finally Ford replied that if he needed to know this information, he knew exactly where to find it. In spite of his weaknesses, Henry Ford was a thinker, a dreamer, and a creator. Today Henry Ford is a household name and his dreams dot the highways of the world. Now I ask you, what were the names of the Tribune editors? Ford said, "An educated man is not one who has trained his mind to retain a few dates in history. He is one who can accomplish things. Unless a man has learned to think, he is not an educated man, regardless of how many college degrees he has after his name."[4]

Utilization of the brain's dormant 95 percent certainly would increase our capacity for conceptualization, visualization, and even faith—a power we are told can move mountains. Certainly there are many abilities of the brain just waiting to be tapped. For example, the human brain has phenomenal memory, reasoning, and deduction capabilities, but it's most extraordinary ability is the power to create. Highly successful individuals employ this creative power of the brain to their advantage.

Is the glass half empty or half full? "Success or failure depends more upon attitude than upon capacity. . . . Successful men act as though they have accomplished or are enjoying something. Soon it becomes a reality. Act, look, feel successful, conduct yourself accordingly, and you will be amazed at the results."[5] If you truly believe in something, you give permission to your wonderful, mystical, and powerful brain to create it.

> Try to fix firmly in your mind what you would like to do; and then, without veering off direction, you will move straight to the goal. Keep

> your mind on the great and splendid things you would like to do; and then, as the days go gliding away, you will find yourself unconsciously seizing upon the opportunities that are required for the fulfillment of your desire. . . . Picture in your mind the able, earnest, useful person you desire to be, and the thought you hold is hourly transforming you into that particular individual. . . . Thought is supreme. Preserve a right mental attitude—the attitude of courage, frankness, and good cheer. To think rightly is to create.[6]

In order for uncommon success to be achieved in life, we must envision it in the mind and then accompany it with belief and action. Conversely, the negative and untrained mind can ball and chain us to a mediocre existence and paralyze us with fear and doubt. The positive mind believes there are no limitations to what it can do. Too many of us have allowed negative reinforcement to saturate our brains with poor programming: "You can't do that. You're not good enough. Don't even try because you're a failure." Soon overwhelming negative self-talk persuades the mind that it is what it thinks. Kahlil Gabran said: "We choose our joys and sorrows long before we experience them."[7]

As I mentioned earlier, in 1999 I became very ill. Because of low spinal fluid pressure, I suffered blinding headaches, dizziness, and sensitivity to light. After months of tests and failed attempts to remedy the problem, the doctors seemed baffled. I had undergone every conceivable test that could be performed. I was worn out from the painful medical marathon. Although the doctors couldn't find what was wrong with me, I was sick and slowly getting sicker. Mentally I was depressed and at my lowest level. I felt I was dying!

During one of my darkest days, I received a personal phone call from a dear and wise friend. From the beginning of my illness he kept in touch, and each time reminded me he had placed my name on the temple prayer roll. "Jeff, how have you been feeling lately?" His voice over the line made me feel as if the darkness broke and the shadows fled.

Tears of comfort filled my eyes, but the obstinate Irish in me wouldn't allow my voice to crack. To my wife's great consternation, I would never tell him just how sick and how much pain I was in. In every instance I would keep my composure and try to put the best spin on my circumstance. "They're not finding what's wrong with me," I replied. Among other things he expressed concern that I hadn't been diagnosed properly.

We chatted for a few moments when he said gently, "Jeff, I want you to do something for me. As difficult as it may be, I want you to smile whenever possible. Even though you don't feel like it, I want you to laugh for no reason at all, and look to the good and wonderful things of your life." He then expressed his love and best wishes and said good-bye.

As he spoke, I remembered these words from another occassion: "I am asking that we stop seeking out the storms and enjoy more fully the sunlight. I am suggesting that as we go through life, we accentuate the positive. I am asking that we look a little deeper for the good, that we still our voices of insult and sarcasm, that we more generously compliment virtue and effort."[8]

I will tell you frankly, I wasn't prepared to hear those words from my friend, and struggled with them for months afterward. Apparently my wife is right, I thought. He doesn't understand how sick I really am or how could he treat my pain and suffering so trivially? I was too sick to realize that he was unaware that I was only a shadow of the strong man he had last seen. Since then the lines in my face had aged years. He had not seen the countless nights my children cried themselves to sleep because they could hear their father in constant agony. He had not been present during those dark nights when I literally pleaded with my wife not to sleep because I was too worn out to face the pain alone. He did not see this father slowly work his way through each room to write affectionate notes on toys and personal effects because he was convinced he would not live to see them the next morning.

Time passed by at a snail's pace, and I wasn't getting any better. In fact, I was getting worse. Fortunately, I thought a lot about this wise man's remarks and out of sheer desperation I slowly began to apply his simple advice. Although the results didn't jump out at me in any grand way, month-by-month, I gradually began to improve.

As I look back on this dark time of my life, it is painfully clear to me that in addition to my breakdown in health, I was my own worst enemy! Due to constant and tremendous pain, I had absolutely convinced myself I was dying. It was as though I had given myself a death sentence and was dutifully going through the motions of doing just that—dying. My body was merely responding to this very convincing stimulus from my brain. It's clear to me that my friend believed in the healing power of the priesthood, which resulted in him putting my name on the temple prayer roll. He understood the healing power of love and showed and expressed it in his calls. It's equally obvious to me that he understood the tremendous power the brain has to either create or destroy, and he knew that until I changed my thinking from negative to positive and began to exercise positive faith, I probably wouldn't get better. "One of the illusions of life is that the present hour is not the critical decisive hour. Write it on your heart that every day is the best day of the year. He only is right who owns the day, and no one owns the day who allows it to be invaded by worry, fret and anxiety. Finish the day, and be done with it. You have done what you could."[9]

Even priesthood blessings require certain conditions to be most effective. Time would prove my friend was correct! Not only did I start getting better when I changed my thinking, the test eventually proved I had no leak in my dural sleeve.

Few people realize they are the masters of their own destiny. Physically you are what you eat, but quite literally you become what you think. Therefore, think positively, believe that you can accomplish anything your heart desires, and think these thoughts often. Your brain must first have complete permission to create your dreams and give them life.

Your words, your dreams, and your thoughts have power to create conditions in your life. What you speak about, you can bring about! If you keep saying you can't stand your job, you might be demoted or even lose your job! If you keep saying you can't stand your body, your body can become sick, infirm, or crippled! If you keep saying you can't stand your car, your car could be stolen, quit operating, or even burn to the ground! If you keep saying you're always broke, guess what, you will always be broke! If you keep saying you cannot trust a man or a woman, you will always find someone in your life to hurt or betray you! If you keep saying you can't find a job, you will always remain unemployed! If you keep saying you can't find someone to love you or to believe in you, you will always remain alone! Our very thoughts will attract more experiences to confirm our beliefs. Turn your thoughts and conversations around to be more positive and power packed with faith, hope, love, and action. Watch your thoughts, they become words; watch your words, they become actions; watch your actions, they become habits; watch your habits, they become your character; watch your character, for it becomes destiny. And try to remember to get out of your own way.

Any positive thought given to the brain becomes a brick in the warehouse of your subconscious. Similarly, every negative thought becomes a pile of sand. When you need a firm foundation upon which to erect your dreams, when your mind searches its resource of building materials, will it find a cache of bricks or a pile of sand? Successful individuals find valuable bricks to build their dreams, but the negative individuals find mostly sand. Therefore, it is imperative you are good to yourself. Stack those positive bricks. You cannot build your dreams on or with sand. "And every one that heareth these sayings of mine, and doeth them not, shall be likened unto a foolish man, which built his house upon the sand: And the rain descended, and the floods came, and the winds blew, and beat upon that house; and it fell: and great was the fall of it" (Matthew 7:26–27).

Our personal habits now become a critical issue. Don't become discouraged if your habits are lacking. Entirely new ones can be developed by utilizing the powerful brick-or-sand process—positive versus negative thinking.

The first step is to begin working as though you do have good habits. You will discover your emerging creation will give you energy and excitement that will aid you in this process of developing better habits. Worthy projects can change our entire outlook on life and make a different person of you. Begin by telling yourself often that you have impeccable habits. After you do this enough you will become what you think.

> I am your constant companion. I am your greatest helper or your heaviest burden. I will push you onward or drag you down to failure. I am completely at your command. Half the things you do, you might just as well turn over to me, and I will be able to do them quickly and correctly. I am easily managed; you must merely be firm with me. Show me exactly how you want something done, and after a few lessons I will do it automatically. I am the servant of all great men, and, alas, of all failures as well. Those who are great, I have made great. Those who are failures, I have made failures. I am not a machine, though I work with all the precision of a machine plus the intelligence of a man. You may run me for profit, or run me for ruin; it makes no difference to me. Take me, train me, be firm with me and I will put the world at your feet. Be easy with me, and I will destroy you. Who am I? I am Habit![10]

With good habits and enough bricks, there is only one obstacle standing between success and us. Fear! Fear is the indisputable paralyzer of unrealized dreams. Fear is purely an illusion of the brain. Because fear is a creation of the brain, it can be overridden or controlled by the brain. "It is life's only true opponent. Only fear can defeat life. It is a clever, treacherous adversary. It has no decency, respects no law or convention, shows no mercy. It goes for your weakest spot, which it finds with unerring ease. It begins in your mind always. Quickly, you make rash decisions. You dismiss your last allies; hope and trust. There, you've defeated yourself. Fear, which is but an impression, has triumphed over you."[11]

In the popular story of the Wizard of Oz, Dorothy and her friends faced their fears and approached the imposing wizard to seek his help. Walking past fear, they approached the belching smoke, flashing lights, and imagery of the intimidating wizard. Dorothy and her friends discovered that the great Wizard of Oz was, in reality, a little old man behind a curtain. Fear is the little man behind a curtain—someone or something that is trying to scare you into inaction. And, just as the Wizard tried to frighten Dorothy from looking behind the curtain, you too can ignore your fear.[12] Remember, only butterflies and weak knees separate you from your dreams.

My young son had been acting timidly for several weeks, and my wife and I had been unsuccessful in determining the reason. One day he came to us in tears and said he would never be able to play or do his outside chores again. After our urging him, he finally confided an ugly, red-headed bully had taken over our farm and chased him every time he went outside. Aware there were no children close by, my wife and I probed deeper and, to our surprise, we discovered the bully was a tom turkey. Apparently it had taken a disliking to our son and would spread his large wings and charge the boy any time he went near the barn. I gave him a stick and told him to go back outside, and if the turkey came at him again, crack it over his head.

"But Poppy," my son said, "that would hurt the turkey."

"Yes," I replied, "but the turkey is out of control and standing between your responsibilities and your fun. You must be brave and face the turkey head-on until it leaves you alone."

My boy bowed his head and reluctantly went outside. After he had run away from the mad turkey several times, and after a lot of coaching from my wife and me, our son finally made a stand. He closed his eyes and swung the stick at the bully with all his might. Stunned and confused, the turkey quickly wobbled away. My boy did it! He managed to face his fear and slew the dragon that had vexed his life. Self-empowered, he was a different boy from that point forward.

"Wise men put their trust in idea and not in circumstance," said Ralph Waldo Emerson.[13] How many of us are paralyzed from achieving our dreams because of belching smoke, flashing lights, and big ugly turkeys in our lives? Like my son and Dorothy, we must march toward our fears and meet them head on; we must battle until our fears are exposed or wobble away. "For God hath not given us the spirit of fear; but of power, and of love, and of a sound mind" (2 Timothy 1:7).

B.C. Forbes said, "Men who have done big things are those who were not afraid to attempt big things, who were not afraid to risk failure in order to gain success."[14] Wonderful and mighty things begin to happen when we unmoor our ships from the safety of the harbor and navigate them out to high seas!

According to Henry J. Kaiser, "What a man can imagine or conceive in his mind he can accomplish. Impossibles are possible as thinking men make them so."[15] In the Old Testament we read, "As a man thinketh in his heart so is he" (Proverbs 23:7).

Therefore, as a lightning rod attracts and directs power in a thunderstorm, the fourteenth amazing treasure is designed to attract and direct positive elements to its benefactor. This treasure can transform, elevate, and create. The treasure reveals:

Conceptualizing is the mystical and wondrous place where creation begins. If the human mind is set free to properly conceive a dream, the dream will one day sprout wings and take flight. Positive elements are unleashed and set into motion when ordinary minds dare to dream and believe. Visualize your success and add to it amazing detail. Give yourself permission to reach for those tiny speckles in the sky! Enthusiastically believe your goals and dreams are possible and within your reach. Believe in yourself; believe in your divine heritage. As a child of God, created in His image, you have divine potential. Open the power of your mind, and you will go places and accomplish things that you never could have imagined. Therefore, "Throw off the bowlines, sail away from the safe harbor. Catch the trade winds in your sails. Explore. Dream. Discover."[16]

Notes

1. "George Bernard Shaw quote," http://www.quotedb.com/quotes/3143.
2. "Jack London's 'Credo,' " http://london.sonoma.edu/credo.html.
3. *The Sound of Music*, DVD, directed by Robert Wise (1965, Hollywood: 20th Century Fox. 2005).
4. Henry Ford quoted by Thomas S. Monson, "Teachings of President Monson," http://www.mormontimes.com/around_church/general_authority/?id=2402.

5. Dupree Jordan, "Daily Quotes," http://lightson.net/quotes2005.htm.
6. "Love, Life & Work by Elbert Hubbard: Mental Attitude," http://www.online-literature.com/elbert-hubbard/love-life-and-work/6/.
7. Kahil Gabran, "Quote World," http://quoteworld.org/quotes/5369
8. Gordon B. Hinckley, "Words of the Prophet: The Spirit of Optimism," *New Era*, Jul. 2001, 4.
9. "Ralph Waldo Emerson—Philosopher-Poet—Poetry," http://www.bella-online.com/articles/art8637.asp.
10. Anonymous, "Focus Quote," http://www.discoversolutions.com/nl/nl_04_2005b.html.
11. Yann Martel, *Life of Pi* (New York: Harcourt, 2001), 161.
12. *The Wizard of Oz*, DVD, directed by Victor Fleming (1939, Hollywood: MGM, 2005).
13. "More quotes by Ralph Waldo Emerson," http://www.answers.com/topic/quote-4?author=Emerson,%20Ralph%20Waldo&s2=Ralph%20Waldo%20Emerson.
14. B.C. Forbes in "BusinessWorld Online: The View from Taft," http://www.bworld.com.ph/BW010809/content.php?id=142.
15. Henry J. Kaiser in *Richard Evans' Quote Book* (Salt Lake City: Publishers Press, 1971), 58.
16. Mark Twain, "Boise State University Health, Wellness and Counseling Services," http://www.boisestate.edu/healthservices/zen/archives.asp.

"Nothing can bring you peace but yourself; nothing can bring you peace but the triumph of principles." —Ralph Waldo Emerson[1]

Amazing Treasure Number Fifteen

Contentment: The Priceless Jewel

"Promise yourself to be so strong that nothing can disturb your peace of mind. . . . To wear a cheerful countenance at all times and give every living creature you meet a smile. . . . To be too large for worry, too noble for anger, too strong for fear, and too happy to permit the presence of trouble."[2]

During the winter of 1984, I was working as a security officer for a downtown campus. Late one night, I received a call on the radio from the Operations and Communications Center concerning men who had been spotted in the shrubs near one of our buildings. I responded and found two transients sitting on the air exhaust grate trying to stay warm through the cold night. One of the two men smiled when I approached and said to his friend, "It looks like it's time for us to move along." The singular scene tugged at my heart. Their sparse worldly possessions consisted of a few worn sacks that they had on their laps. Their ages were difficult to determine due to their weatherworn faces, but they appeared elderly. As they nervously gathered their belongings, I held up my hand and gestured them to remain seated. The worried looks subsided. In my stern security voice, I told them they were welcome to stay if they promised to leave the premises as clean and orderly as they had found them. They both promised, and I turned and began to walk away. Then one of the men called out to me. "What is your name, sir?"

"Jeffrey Hair," I replied.

"God bless you, Jeffrey Hair," he said softly.

Through the years, I came to know this fellow as Happy Hutchinson. He loved Salt Lake City and visited every chance he could. Freight trains were his mode of transportation, and the stars his roof. Each time I encountered Happy, I became more intrigued. I learned to love Happy Hutchinson

Despite his dismal circumstances, he was one of the most contented individuals I had ever known. He once pulled from his backpack a worn and weathered copy of The Book of Mormon and recounted for me his conversion. He freely enumerated his weaknesses, but his voice always cracked when he bore testimony of the restored gospel. I have heard powerful testimonies in great halls, but I have seldom been more touched than by the heartfelt testimony of a ragged old homeless man on a side street of Salt Lake City.

The last time I saw Happy was on a planter box in front of the Church Administration Building. We hadn't seen each other for several years, so we had a lot of catching up to do. I was married by then and had three children. He asked me if I had a picture of my family. I pulled out my wallet and handed it to him. He took it as if he had been handed something extremely precious or delicate. He carefully opened it and looked at the little family photo with a deep and penetrating gaze. As he studied the photograph, tears began to well up in his eyes, and he motioned me to sit down next to him. He said, "What a lucky and blessed man you are, Jeffrey Hair. You have such a beautiful family. Promise me you won't do as I did and let these little ones get away from you." He explained that the majority of people living on the streets have little choice in the matter due to mental illnesses or handicaps. He, on the other hand, had chosen his path by poor decisions. "Out on the street," he said, "there were so many lost and lonely people who needed love, direction, and encouragement. I have never had the heart to leave them. I suppose this is my mission in life—I am Father Transient. I wouldn't recommend it though; it's a hard and dangerous life." And then he laughed as he proceeded to show me his battle wounds.

The curtain of our eternal possibilities has been raised, and while heaven and angels watch with anticipation, we act out our brief life on the great stage of mortality. This is it! The earth is filled with artifacts and tombs from past civilizations, but today is our time and our turn to live. The scriptures teach plainly that God's purpose for us is that we might have joy, yet so many of us are consumed in a haze of discontent. Isn't it ironic that I should learn some of the greatest lessons about happiness from a man who lived on the streets? Happy Hutchinson had more reason to be unhappy in a day's experiences than most of us do in a lifetime, yet he never wasted a precious moment complaining. He loved life and discovered riches that many of us can only dream about. He was a father figure and lovingly nurtured the homeless. Not all wealth can be measured by the mighty dollar. Those who have been wise enough to find this elusive principle are among the happiest people who have ever lived.

Elder Jones was a man who wasn't content with anything. Although he was eventually assigned to be an assistant to the president, he became consumed with envy toward his fellow companion who was his senior. After he returned home, he continued to try and prove superiority over his rival. He became consumed with financial success. Sadly, every time I ran into Elder Jones, he rambled on about his accomplishments. On one occasion, he was standing with several associates when he asked me in a condescending tone what I had accomplished since my mission. Before I could answer, he proceeded to introduce me to each of his associates. When he had finished, he boasted that each of them worked for him in a premium office in an elite part of town. Apparently it was not enough! With all he had he was still not content. Shortly after our brief visit, he began to embezzle money from friends and investors. Eventually he lost his wife and family and wound up in a federal prison for several years.

Even worth billions, Sam Walton understood the simple but true recipe for contentment. He said, "Money never has meant that much to me, not even in the sense of keeping score. If we had enough groceries, and a nice place to live, plenty of room to keep and feed my bird dogs, a place to hunt, a place to play tennis, and the means to get the kids a good education—that's rich. . . . I still can't believe it was news that I get my haircut at the barbershop. Where else would I get it cut? Why do I drive a pickup truck? What am I supposed to haul my dogs around in, a Rolls-Royce?"[3] Sam understood the principle of contentment. He was unpretentious with others and found simple pleasure in the little things of life.

Contentment is very different from apathy. Apathy is lazy, indifferent, and spiritless, while contentment speaks of peace, gratitude, and thankfulness. Contentment realizes if you don't have peace within yourself, it is useless to seek it from an exterior source. Contentment strives to enjoy each moment in spite of circumstances. Apathy waits for the perfect moments. Contentment gives color to life, while apathy robs life of meaning and purpose. Without contentment, a man could literally own the treasures of earth and he would perpetually reside in a state of torment, loneliness, and misery.

Contentment doesn't mean we can't strive to better our lot in life, but we must carefully guard against the tendency to be consumed by it. Live, love, and enjoy life today.

Ezra Taft Benson warned us never to become a victim of the sin of ingratitude.[4] Ingratitude breeds discontent. It covets that which is not its own. It keeps score and isn't thankful for anything.

> And as he entered into a certain village, there met him ten men that were lepers, which stood afar off: And they lifted up their voices, and said, Jesus, Master, have mercy on us. And when he saw them, he said unto them, Go shew yourselves unto the priests. And it came to pass, that, as they went, they were cleansed. And one of them, when he saw that he was healed, turned back, and with a loud voice glorified God. And fell down on his face at his feet, giving him thanks; and he was a Samaritan. And Jesus answering said, Were there not ten cleansed? But where are the nine? There are not found that returned to give glory to God, save this stranger. And he said unto him, Arise, go thy way: thy faith hath made thee whole (Luke 17:12–19).

Praise to the Samaritan leper! Something whispers to me he found contentment in his life. It is difficult to comprehend that he represented only 10 percent of those who had been healed of the terrible scourge of leprosy. He alone returned to give thanks to the Healer. The numbers used by the Lord in this parable may be significant. Could it be possible that 90 percent of us display too little gratitude for our blessings?

Gratitude has a beautiful twin sister named "Thankfulness." If given proper attention, they will help us cultivate contented hearts. It is learning to be content with limited material possessions that leads us to the creation of a new folder in our portfolio called: Greater Happiness and Joy Today. Gratitude sheds happiness on those who embrace her, thankfulness is the heartfelt recognition of God's love and blessings in our lives.

"How sharper than a serpent's tooth it is to have a thankless child" King Lear said.[5] My children know I expect a display of gratitude and a true appreciation for life and the many blessings they have been given. Brigham Young taught, "I do not know of any, excepting the unpardonable sin that is greater than the sin of ingratitude."[6] Perhaps this is true because ingratitude appears to accompany all other sins.

Parents should take the opportunity to share with children the disparity of wealth that exists in the world today. I have found an occasional family visit to a homeless shelter is a powerful and an invaluable teaching device. Before visiting, each child picks a favorite toy to add to the blankets and food to be donated.

Occasionally we visit a pioneer cabin to experience firsthand how our ancestors lived. We have learned to appreciate what few possessions and comforts they enjoyed. None of our children will forget the trip we took to Mexico. We saw the countless miles of shanties that lined the streets. My children could scarcely believe that families lived in these boarded huts. But they do live there. Similarly, I know of a wise but poor mother of ten children who bakes bread and has her children deliver the loaves to the homeless and the needy in their neighborhood.

Previously, we discussed the general unhappiness of the extremely wealthy. I would like to share with you an unusual dream that taught me a profound lesson. I dreamed I had been taken on a tour of two huge mansions. My escort was an employee of the man who owned both of them. The opulence of these homes was disturbing to both my tour guide and me. On several occasions, we discussed the magnificence and seeming unfairness of it all. We would say things like, "Can you believe it, nobody needs to live like this. What an ostentatious display of money."

What further amazed us was that the mansions were so close in proximity. As we mused, we scratched our heads. Why would anyone need even one mansion, let alone two that were only several minutes from each other? We were overwhelmed at what we witnessed. I began to feel angry. This money could have gone for much better causes! My escort confirmed my feelings when he confided that the owner was indeed self-absorbed. I couldn't stand it any longer. I wanted to know the name of the owner. "Jeffrey Hair!" was his reply. We must remember wealth can be relative. Although my homes are nowhere near mansions by our modern standards, they could appear this way to those living in third world countries.

The average American lives a life of luxury that yesterday's kings would envy. Compared to horse-drawn chariots, our chariots move at supersonic speeds across land and sky. Our life expectancy is twice what ancient peoples could expect. Compare a Shakespeare stage production with today's surround-sound action movie on the big screen. Through modern technology and the harnessing of electricity, even the relatively poor among us can command the forces of comfort and convenience.

Think of the luxury of central air conditioning, for example. Consider the miracle of making a phone call and having a pizza delivered within minutes. Clearly, we live more comfortably than the royals of yesteryear.

Sadly, it is not enough! We are no happier than they were. The principle of contentment requires that we see our blessings and ourselves in the backdrop of history. We are among the most blessed people who have ever lived. At no time have the most impoverished among us had so much freedom and enjoyed so many comforts. Have you ever struggled just to breathe? (I did for several months.) Can you walk or run? Are you loved—do you love someone? Have your arms held a newborn child? Can you see? Do you appreciate the beauty all around you? Can you hear the many sounds of life—the call of a robin in the morning? Is your stomach full? Do you live the balance of your life in freedom? Are you fortunate enough to have a mission that occupies your time and thoughts? Do you have a job? Do you have trials that challenge you to the very core? Do you have a dream? Have you ever been so happy you've cried? Have you ever felt God's love?

My dear friend Happy, despite how some may view you, I see so clearly that your life has purpose and meaning. I wish I were more like you and possessed that innocent, childlike faith. I wish I could more freely express my sins and weaknesses—my love to others, as you do. One day I hope to see materialism through your eyes. Wherever you are, Happy, thanks for showing me you don't have to own much of anything to find sublime contentment here on earth. God bless you. You are among my heroes.

Is it any wonder "Happy the Transient" revealed the fifteenth amazing treasure? He captured this fleeting, shooting star of human emotion in a mason jar and liberally shared it with all in need.

Under every stone we move and every bead of sweat we perspire, contentment can be discovered along the journey of life. Notwithstanding, in order to achieve this most priceless commodity we must be true to ourselves. As Abraham Lincoln said, "I desire so to conduct [my] affairs . . . that if at the end . . . I have lost every other friend on earth, I shall at least have one friend left, and the friend shall be down inside of me." Hence, I already possess what I need to be like Happy.

Notes

1. Ralph Waldo Emerson, "Goodreads," http://www.goodreads.com/quotes/show/38023.
2. "The Optimist Creed," http://www.optimist.org/default.cfm?content=Vistors/visitors.htm.

3. Sam Walton, *Sam Walton, Made in America* (New York: Doubleday, 1992), 7.
4. Ezra Taft Benson, "Receive All Things with Thankfulness," *New Era*, Nov. 1976, 4.
5. William Shakespeare, "King Lear," Act I, Scene 4, http://shakespeare.mit.edu/lear/full.html.
6. Brigham Young, *Teachings of the Presidents of the Church: Brigham Young* (Salt Lake City: Intellectual Reserve), 177.
7. Abraham Lincoln, "QuotationsBook," http://quotationsbook.com/quote/16178/.

"For which of you, intending to build a tower, sitteth not down first, and counteth the cost, whether he have sufficient [funds] to finish it? Lest haply, after he hath laid the foundation, and is not able to finish it, all that behold it begin to mock him, saying, this man began to build, and was not able to finish." Luke 14:28–30

Amazing Treasure Number Sixteen

Strategy: The Ultimate Dream Catcher

Fight to win! Fight with a strategy! You must "know your enemy and know yourself; had you then a hundred wars to fight, you would be a hundred times victorious."[1] A great general would never consider marching his men into battle without a carefully designed plan.

Early in my life, I learned that a person or team with a well-constructed strategy has the definite advantage. According to Merriam-Webster's Dictionary, strategy is "the art of devising or employing plans or stratagems toward a goal."[2] I like to think of a good strategy as a plan with a sharp edge.

I can't think of a faster way to bondage and unfulfilled dreams than to travel through life without a plan. Can you imagine such a mentality? It would be equivalent to Napoleon the Great blindly charging at his enemy's fortification in an ad hoc manner, while shooting from the hip. Working without a strategy is tantamount to searching for treasure without a map.

A few years ago a monetarily sound friend of mine, Jared, received an assignment from his bishop to assist a ward family in digging out of a deep financial hole. This family had struggled on and off for many years and received substantial assistance from the ward. As the meeting developed, Jared learned that the father made very good money and the biggest problem facing the family was the absence of a working budget. Jared never did get over the shock of discovering that the family's income was almost double his own! The difference was that one family had a working budget and the other did not.

An effective budgetary strategy will help you create a list of prioritized needs to guide you through the endless maze of impulse and emotion buying. For example: securing a substantial down payment on a home before you purchase a newer car or take an exotic vacation. Maybe new cabinets, carpet, and appliances can wait until your home's mortgage is paid in full.

A good strategy takes advantage of and incorporates personal strengths. An eagle loses its advantage when it is forced from the sky to compete with turkeys and chickens on the ground. Conversely, turkeys and chickens are poor opponents to the eagle in the sky. Such competition is poor strategy. In order to strategize effectively, you must know who and what you are; you must know your strengths and weaknesses, and you must learn to exploit those strengths effectively.

For example, someone who is unusually good with people might consider finding a good product to sell. I dearly love music and especially enjoy world-class vocals. Some of my favorites include Mario Lonza and The Three Tenors. However, no matter how many voice lessons I take, no matter what I gargle, and no matter how many throat surgeries I undergo, my family would starve to death if I was determined to sing for a living. But I am gifted in the field of finance, and in this pursuit I have wings. As a result, my family has done well. Finance is a strength that separates me from the masses. Here in the sky I am not competing with turkeys and chickens on the ground.

Patience ensures that we are prepared to take advantage when opportunities knock. After all, Fortune favors the best prepared people.

Start the process by keeping meticulous books and chart every penny that comes in or goes out. I will never forget my mission president, Sloan Alma Smith, who spent hours searching for a few lost pennies in the mission's balance sheets. I asked him why he spent so much time tracking down a few pennies. "If the balance sheet is off by a few pennies," he said, "the accuracy of the entire account will always be in question." He explained that any mistake made in the accounting, even by a few cents, could mark the possibility of more significant errors.

In a very real sense, you are the CEO and president of your family's finances, and like any good CEO, you need to know exactly where your money is and where it is going. Here again, keep it simple. It has been wisely stated, "Simplicity of character [or strategy] is the natural result of profound thought." Knowing and understanding the facts is powerful information for any CEO; and it is extremely difficult to make good decisions without accurate and necessary information.

After we married, my wife and I moved into a nice apartment in Holladay, Utah. Every dollar we made was spent on rent, car repairs, insurance, and bills. When the first month ended, we had no extra money to put into savings. We thought we were scrimping in every way we could. A few months went by and things didn't get better. All we were doing was working to make ends meet. We were getting nowhere. It became clear to us that we would never own a home or build a sound financial foundation if something didn't change.

Three months after we moved into our apartment, my wife and I sat down in the "war room" and put everything on the table. We didn't hold back on possessions or habits. Everything underwent scrutiny. After long and serious deliberation, we came to understand that we needed to develop a financial plan for winning or we would go nowhere; we would lose.

Our line of attack included an intense period of saving and preparation that would last for a few years while we were both young and employed. According to our plan, we sold our only car and my motorcycle. We put the money in a savings account. Then we moved into a tiny apartment, which cost a fourth of the price of our nice one. We didn't even allow ourselves the luxury of a phone for a while. Our apartment was located about half a mile from a bus stop. For the next few years, we rode the bus for transportation.

This was a time of magic for us; we believed in our plan and that gave us the motivation to persevere. We were making progress, and it was our little secret. When we had saved a $1,000, we treated ourselves to a $1.99 special at Arctic Circle. It was the most satisfying dinner I have ever eaten. When we reached $5,000, we treated ourselves to a dollar movie and another Arctic Circle special. It was even more satisfying than the first.

We loved and invested in each other. We were creative on our dates and avoided spending money. We went on long walks, hikes in the mountains, and rode the bus into town to sightsee and window shop. Sometimes we just sat back and dreamed about our future, what we hoped to accomplish and where we wanted to live.

As the money began to accumulate, literally hundreds of opportunities were presented to us to spend or invest our savings for material things or high-stake ventures, but we resisted. After a couple of years, we had saved tens of thousands of dollars. We used some of the money for a down payment on a home. After moving into the home, we managed to keep up the pace. We paid off the thirty-year mortgage and started a business, all within six years.

Incidentally, we were so relieved to finally reach our goals of paying off the mortgage and starting a business that we relaxed and stopped following a budget. Months went by and we discovered to our dismay that we hadn't saved a dime. So you see, nobody can tell me a budget is ineffective! Since then, we've returned to our strategy and put our budget back in place, and we are so much more effective.

What a relief to look back! We prepared and sewed seeds during the springtime of our lives. We will never again worry about being homeless or scraping together a mortgage payment every month. We have extra money for family and fun and of course, for savings.

To begin with, analyze your current situation. Gather facts about such things as income, insurance, debt, savings, retirement planning, schooling, goals, and priorities. Ask yourself tough questions. Where are you now and where do you want to be in five or ten years?

Create new financial goals and strategies. Remember your goals must be based upon hard numbers and facts. If or when magic should bless your life, it must be considered an extra and not included in your goals. Goals should be as specific and measurable as possible. The goal to save fifteen thousand dollars in five years is more specific than the decision to put money into a savings account. A deadline should be attached to each goal so success can be measured.

How are you going to come up with extra money to put away, by spending less or making more? Are you family-oriented? If so, you may decide to cut back on spending rather than spending more time working.

Execute your plan and start as soon as possible. President Kimball was fond of saying, "Just do it!" You may need to revise your goals and strategies as changes in your circumstances occur. When old goals and dreams are realized, new ones should be created.

The majority of people fail to see that with just a little determination they can improve their entire life! The following are among the most common excuses I've heard, followed by a brief rebuttal:

Excuse 1: I don't earn enough money to make ends meet—it's physically impossible. So why even try?

The vast majority of people make enough money to live comfortably—they just manage their money poorly. As sad as it this may sound, middle-class Americans are their own worst enemies regarding personal finance. I would be the wealthiest man on the planet if I had a dime for every time someone in the middle class uttered the phrase, "It takes money to make money." Have you heard someone say this? Sadly, it is used to justify our predicament. Too often it serves as a convenient excuse to remain there. This declaration is usually followed with an observation that supports the premise like, "Joe bought the land for pennies on the dollar, sat on it for several months, and sold it for a huge profit. You know, if I had that kind of money I could do the same thing." If your situation is typical, there are literally hundreds of thousands of penny soldiers, which with a little effort, could be squeezed out of your monthly expenditures. If you are determined, you'll find a way to have discretionary funds to bless your life. If there is any one thing out there that can universally elevate the working class and give them a better life, it is a budget that places expenditures below income. Remember, the buck stops with you. Absolutely do not allow present circumstances to dictate your future.

Excuse 2: I'm not disciplined enough to make a budget work.

Grab the wheel of your ship, control your money, or very soon its absence will control you. My experience suggests that if you don't have a budget, you are likely in debt. A ship without a captain attentively at the wheel will ultimately end up crushed upon the reef. Anyone who has enough regiment to hold down a job can work an effective budget. I promise it is not that involved or complicated! Once a budget is effectively utilized, you'll never go back to the ad hoc method of living, spending, and paying obligations. In fact, you will wonder how you managed without one. It should be noted that the undisciplined need a budget more than the disciplined.

Excuse 3: I like spontaneity and a budget is stifling

Karen is a true yellow if ever I knew one. If a friend yelled out, "Hey, who wants to go to California with me tomorrow," Karen would immediately sign up. She would then go and have an absolutely wonderful time. It is only after she returns home and begins to receive bills that she wonders how to pay for them. Because she is already overwhelmed with debt, she tosses it aside and avoids dealing with the consequence of her actions. Since she refused to discipline herself through her teens and twenties, she brought debt and misery into a marriage. Unfortunately for both of them, her husband is the same way. Can you imagine the condition of their finances and the extreme stress it causes? There is no other word to describe it—it's hell! Spontaneity is fun at parties, but keep it out of your financial affairs.

Excuse 4: A budget infringes upon my freedom. It's too restrictive.

America has recently come to appreciate the high cost of freedom. It's one of those significant things in our lives that are absolutely worth protecting. Therefore, remember this: few things are more restrictive than poor credit and excessive debt. In fact, like living the gospel, the entire purpose for incorporating a budget is to maximize your freedom and happiness, not limit it!

Excuse 5: I'm lousy at numbers.

Maybe so, but I'll bet you can integrate the simple envelope system. This technique involves dividing your paycheck up into envelopes; one for each monthly bill—including flush and savings funds. If there is not enough money to cover expenses, something will have to be cut. Remember Spencer W. Kimball's comment about achieving according to the simplicity of your efforts? Some of my colleagues advocate rather complicated budget formulas that take into account every present and future need. Personally, I like to keep it as simple as humanly possible.

Excuse 6: The financial hole I've dug is too deep to work a budget. Just thinking about it depresses me.

The deeper in debt people are, the more paralyzed they become. If you experience even the smallest desire to become debt-free, it is imperative you act upon it immediately. Very few situations are terminal. Consider the true story of a seemingly ordinary fellow from Bentonville, Arkansas, who jumped headlong into the retailing business. After five years of fumbling and working hard, he lost his store due to a bad lease agreement. Refusing to give up, he and his wife moved to another town and started over. Within a few years he opened two new stores—one of which was totally destroyed by lightning. Even with these disappointments, he kept trying and didn't give up.

Listen to what a colleague had to say about an encounter with this fellow from Bentonville:

> In those days, word was starting to get out that a [particular] guy had some interesting retailing ideas, so I drove down from Springfield, where I was with Crank Drugs at the time, to see [one of his store] openings. It was the worst retail store I had ever seen. [The owner] had brought a couple of trucks of watermelons in and stacked them on the sidewalk. He had a donkey ride out in the parking lot. It was about 115 degrees, and the watermelons began to pop, and the donkey began to do what donkeys do, and it all mixed together and ran all over the parking lot. And when you went inside the store, the mess just continued, having been tracked in all over the floor. He was a nice fellow, but I wrote him off. It was just terrible.[3]

As mentioned earlier, within his lifetime Sam Walton would become the most successful merchant in the history of the business and the wealthiest man in the world. The store opening referred to above was none other than Sam's first Walmart. So you see, just because you have a less than ideal situation doesn't mean there is no hope. You will only fail if you lie down and stop trying. Giving up is not among your options. Keep at it! By so doing you will eventually get it right.

Excuse 7: I'm young; right now I want to be free and have a good time. I'll worry about budgeting and money when I'm older.

In reality, there is no better time to practice the art of budgeting than in your youth. Shortly after their marriage, Barry and Lisa treated themselves to a several week cruise halfway around the world. They rationalized that they would never get another chance after children blessed their lives. To make matters worse, both had recently graduated from college and accumulated hefty student loans. Just a few weeks after the trip the suntans faded and souvenirs were placed on shelves or in storage. The stories had been told and retold. I wonder if they understand the loss in their future will be much greater than the approximate $15,000 they actually borrowed to finance the trip. It could set them back for many years. Remember? The key to breaking the middle-class mentality of living from paycheck to paycheck is to do things in the correct order. Every dollar put aside in our youth will duplicate itself time and time again. This little miracle is called compounding interest. When we borrow, we not only pay interest, but we also lose the compounding that occurs from saving.

Excuse 8: My money is gone after I pay the bills. I know all about budgets, but why should I waste my time when my expenses govern me?

Nothing will ever change until you begin to budget. After reading this book, an associate of mine said to me that he enjoyed my book—that it was a "good read." He also explained that after his wife read the book she half jokingly commented that she didn't feel any different—that it didn't change her life as it promised. How would she know whether or not it had that capability if she didn't put into practice any of its principles?

Although I'm flattered that they enjoyed the book, it is not simply a good read. The power behind a budget and these twenty-one amazing treasures is not so much about intellectually grasping them as it is about applying them—living them.

Excuse 9: I pay my tithing, so everything will work out without a budget.

Unfortunately, this attitude is common and I believe it is one of the reasons behind Utah's high bankruptcy rates. I like to remember that Malachi's promise was made at a time of extreme hardship and primitive circumstances. These people didn't have large beautiful homes, air-conditioning, electricity, running water, automobiles, and the many other modern conveniences we enjoy today. Furthermore, unlike our present circumstances, survival occupied much of their day and when it was over they had precious little time for leisure. Again, most of us live like the kings from that era. It is my firm conviction that the Lord's promises to His people made in Malachi are, for the most part, being fulfilled today, especially in the United States. Strictly materially speaking, should we expect any more from the Lord than we've already been given? It must also be noted that in order to receive the blessings of success in any field of endeavor, we must first obey the laws and principles governing it.

I know an impressive man named Roy Thomson who runs a cattle ranch in northeastern Utah. While convalescing from my illness, Roy would pick me up in his forty-year-old Ford truck to accompany him while he fed his cattle. Although well maintained, his truck, tractors, and equipment showed the fatigue of years of demanding labor. But what he had he owned outright—including his home. He operated his ranch differently than some of the others who were not at all averse to signing away the ranch equity for the latest truck or tractor. Many of these ranchers were tithe payers too, yet who do you think enjoyed the greater financial freedom and peace of mind?

Excuse 10: I'm too busy to worry about a budget.

Once the initial setting up is completed, a budget requires very little time to maintain. I promise the hour or so spent each month in this effort will yield more success than anything else you could do in the same amount of time.

Excuse 11: I plan on making a lot more money in the future. I'll catch up and implement a budget then.

The dream may happen, but there is a possibility it may not. Therefore, as the saying goes, "Don't count your chickens before they hatch." Furthermore, the earlier in life you apply these principles, the more potent the end results will be. I credit the integrating of these principles early in my youth to the comfortable position I enjoy today. My situation wouldn't be as fortunate if I had delayed their implementation. It is easier to save penny soldiers when you're young, and it provides plenty of critical time for these little workers to reproduce themselves.

Excuse 12: I kind of have a working budget in my head. I ease up on spending when I get too far in the hole.

I must say, this method is better than no plan at all. At least there are some built-in checks and balances. But, I would suggest improving and maximizing your strategy by thinking it through and writing it down. How does the saying go? "If it's not written, it's only a wish."

Excuse 13: I have no credit card debt. I make good money—all of our expenses are more than covered.

I know a couple who started out married life following a well-thought-out budget and strategy. Having eliminated consumer debt, they were in the process of paying off their mortgage early. That is until Albert started a new job, which paid twice as much as the old one. In time, both partners relaxed and stopped following a budget. Is it any wonder this family struggles more financially today than they did with half the income?

Excuse 14: A budget is like a New Year's resolution: everybody makes them and nobody keeps them.

What can I say? The alternative is continued frustration and deeper debt. I can't help someone who is unwilling to pick up a sword and fight his battle. There will always be those who lose the conflict without ever firing a single shot! This rationalization is a poor-man's mentality; financially successful people utilize budgets! Hence, the rich get richer and the poor get poorer.

Excuse 15: My parents managed without a budget. What was good enough for Mom and Dad is good enough for me.

First of all, times are different today than they were forty years ago. During your parents' era, debt had a negative stigma and a loan was much harder to obtain. As a result, the average family accumulated very little consumer debt compared with today. Furthermore, if your parents made ends meet, imagine where they might be if they had utilized a budget.

Excuse 16: I don't want my children to be cheated or deny them what I see other children experience.

A widow I was advising defended her over-expenditures because she did not want her children to feel cheated or poor, so when they asked for money she usually gave it to them. Beyond the danger of more debt, what is this teaching the children? This is an oft-repeated concern I hear from parents. Naturally we desire to give our children what they want, but we must resist the temptation! We can seriously cripple them when we don't share family resource limitations. We must teach children that there is no such thing as a money tree. We must be cautious about overly protecting children from difficult struggles that strengthened us. "Affliction is a treasure, and scarce any man hath enough of it. No man hath affliction enough that is not matured and ripened by it and made fit for God."[4]

A universally held "sacred cow" among parents is the extracurricular activities of their children. In righteous pursuit of the quintessential "eleventh commandment" which Moses somehow forgot to record, we religiously cart our children to art lessons, soccer, baseball, football, dance, choir, karate, gymnastics, and piano as if eternal progression depends upon it. The monetary cost can be enormous. Furthermore, these things can be good in moderation, but we should guard against crowding out family time. Sometimes we must choose between "good things" versus "eternal things." No matter what hoops we have our children jumping through, it will not compensate for failure and, I might add, time spent together in the home. After all, "it may be that the worst thing we can give our children is the opportunity to participate in an additional sport, music lesson, or other activity that demands money and time away from the family. Teaching our children how to live 'quiet, sane' and balanced lives may be one of the most vital things we can do for them in these frenzied last days."[5]

But enough with the excuses.

In the nation's White House is a room entitled the "War Room." It is here that the leaders of this nation have plotted and planned strategies to fight the wars they have waged. Each of us, in essence, is fighting our own personal war with debt, desire, and materialism, and need such a place as a war room. It is here you will craft your future success or failure, your heaven or your hell. Don't forget to begin each planning session with prayer.

Like the President consulting his joint chiefs of staff, you too must invite your closest, most respected advisor, your spouse, to be with you in the war room. Remember to leave emotions outside the door because some of the decisions will be very difficult and will affect the entire family.

Let's review again, as these points cannot be belabored. In order to wage effective warfare against a worthy opponent, a general needs soldiers; the more soldiers under your command, the better your chances for victory! The available soldiers to fight your crucial battle of freedom are the undedicated pennies you own, after expenses. This is not your gross income. Therefore, if you make $400,000 a year and at the end of the month—after paying bills—you have only one penny remaining, my friend, you command only one soldier.

But don't dismay! New and fresh troops can be squeezed out of monthly bills by eliminating unnecessary wants and extravagances. After honest evaluation, ax the fat! Then count the hundreds of thousands of new soldiers who will now move at your command. Again, the deeper the cuts, the more soldiers you'll command, and the more effective your fight against the enemy will be!

Next, like Sherman marching through the South, torch and burn the adversary. You do this by directing your soldiers to march on the enemy's weakest stronghold—your smallest debt. Hit it with overwhelming, decisive firepower and resolve. Week after week, month after month, bombard the enemy's position. When the walls of the fort finally crumble, take no prisoners! After the smoke and dust settles revealing the victory, the soldiers who had been previously tied up with this skirmish merely trading punches with the enemy can now join in the crusade to free other soldiers. Subsequently, pick the next weakest stronghold and charge again! Keep in mind that as your army grows, the power over your oppressor grows. Remember too, you are at war!

Keep your gunpowder dry by daily strengthening your resolve! Never let your enemy's presence become commonplace. Never relax after victories for you could lose your will and allow the enemy to regroup. When you win a conflict, celebrate the victory by destroying the credit card. And then, with flag in hand, charge another Bunker Hill.

The proper behavior of a good general requires that he sacrifice with the troops on the battlefield, much like George Washington with his troops at Valley Forge. During the heat of the battle, the general must never be seen indulging himself with expensive extravagances such as movies, nights out on the town, and expensive living quarters. He must lead by example—always motivating the family and troops through his own sacrifices.

In time, you and your troops will be ready to move on to your own personal Gettysburg—the mortgage. Month by month, year after year, send in those troops by making double or triple principle payments. When my wife and I first started to assault our mortgage, every extra fifty dollars we added to the payment saved us approximately six hundred dollars in interest—that's 60,000 troops rescued from certain annihilation, saved to fight for you again and again. Month after month, we hit this stronghold with as many troops as we could afford until finally, after six years of siege and bombardment, the show of force paid off and our mortgage fell. For us it was a crash heard around the world. The total troops liberated were well over ten million dollars!

The key to remember is that you can capture your dreams by thinking them through and writing them down. If I want to accomplish something substantial, something meaningful in my life, I always begin by reaching for a pad of paper and a pencil and creating it conceptually. If you take the time to record and organize your dreams and goals into a strategy, the chances of realizing them rise significantly. As the saying goes, "If you don't know where you are going, any road will take you there."

Thus, the sixteenth amazing treasure was gently lifted from the tarnished chest, its aged and brittle parchment carefully unrolled for earthly throngs to gather and again partake of its wisdom and bounty: It read:

If you fail to plan, you plan to fail. Success and achievement belong to those who prepare for it. A chartered course enlightens and tells us where we are in the grand scheme of things; it reveals where we are in relationship to our present direction. It contains self-imposed rules of monetary conduct. A strategy clarifies the vagueness of our dreams, pulls them from the clouds, and gives us something concrete to work toward. It discriminates between the real things we want and the thousands of things that tug at our time and pocket book.

Go forth now upon your white horse. I bid you Godspeed in the critical war that awaits you and your soldiers. If you would be a general, be a good general and follow a good plan. Lead as though the future of your posterity depends upon this victory. From the bellowing dust and smoke, pledge this day that your flag of peace and prosperity shall one day rise on the highest peak of the land. What a fine day that will surely be.

Notes

1. "Sun Tzu quotes," http://thinkexist.com/quotation/know_your_enemy_and_know_yourself_and_you_can/149703.html
2. "Strategy," http://www.merriam-webster.com/dictionary/strategy
3. Sam Walton, *Sam Walton, Made in America* (New York: Doubleday, 1992).
4. "John Donne Quotes," http://www.brainyquote.com/quotes/quotes/j/johndonne154216.html.
5. Brent L. Top, "A Balanced Life," *Liahona*, Apr. 2005, 40.

"The highest reward for man's toil is not what he gets for it, but what he becomes by it." —John Ruskin[1]

Amazing Treasure Number Seventeen

Sweat & Toil: The Most Powerful Tools Known to Man

After reading my book, a young friend took some time to reflect on his life. He said he has come to regret that his mother did practically everything for her children, including picking up after them. Under her personal philosophy, it was easier to do the work herself than stand over her children and teach them. He said he never realized how badly it crippled him until he landed a real job. One of his first assignments was to wash a company truck. After brief instructions from his supervisor, he filled a bucket with hot sudsy water and headed toward the truck. Not sure where to begin, he stood there for a few minutes paralyzed!

With his boss looking on, out of sheer desperation he wet a corner of the rag and began to meticulously wash a small panel. After a few minutes of rubbing, the boss impatiently interjected this was no way to wash a truck and bade him to get out of the way. To my friend's embarrassment, the boss grabbed the hose from him and wet down the truck. He dunked the rag into the bucket, watery suds splashing everywhere, and threw it onto the truck, moving his arm in large, fast circular motions until the entire surface had been covered, and then grabbed the hose again and quickly rinsed the truck. At this point my friend realized he was approaching adulthood with a serious handicap. In the years since he has worked hard to compensate for this childhood deficiency. He explained the laziest person he knows is lurking beneath his skin, and he has to constantly push himself to stay ahead of him.

The doors of opportunity open to those who are determined and searching for them. Of what significance is opportunity to a lazy man who isn't prepared to grab a pick, shovel, or hammer and brave the heat, dust, or whatever to use it? Tagore wrote, "I slept and dreamt that life was a joy. I woke and saw that life was a service. I acted, and behold the service was a joy."[2]

It was my observation that the dignitaries I worked with shared a few habits in common. They were early risers; they were governed by uncommon discipline; they enjoyed hard work. They were among the first to arrive at the office. Their schedules were long and grueling—especially considering some of their elderly ages. A particularly impressive CEO had aged into his nineties. He dearly loved his home in the country. Here he could get away from the responsibility and pressures of his position and relax if he chose. However, the relaxing didn't last long before he was working on a project somewhere on the little farm. On slower days he expressed a little frustration about his inability to work as long and hard as he did in his seventies. Once he and his wife and I were sitting on the porch when he sighed and said, "Oh, I'm a tired old man, Jeff; but it's a good tired!" He sighed again and was quiet. I studied them and smiled. There he sat with his little wife. She could almost always be found with a smile. Both seemed enshrouded with a glow. With decades of hard work and service beneath their belt, they approached every day with a love for life and an unshakable testimony and commitment to what they believed. I found myself extremely proud and maybe even a bit envious.

> It is interesting that the first recorded instruction given to Adam after the Fall dealt with the eternal principle of work. The Lord said: "In the sweat of they face shalt thou eat bread" (Genesis 3:19). Our Heavenly Father loves us so completely that he has given us a commandment to work. This is one of the keys to eternal life. He knows that we will learn more, grow more, achieve more, serve more, and benefit more from a life of industry than from a life of ease.[3]

Years ago I crossed paths with an interesting individual. I had advertised an opening for a rental apartment and was accepting applications. I was awaiting an appointment when a fancy light blue Cadillac pulled into the long dirt driveway. The driver was talking on a cell phone and I had to wait several minutes for him to complete his conversation. (It must be noted that this was years ago when only the most successful businessmen owned cell phones.) Can you imagine my astonishment to discover he wanted to rent my humble apartment for his family? Within a few days,

Frank Porrage and his little family moved in.

By trade, Frank was a steel fabricator. During the few times he was actually employed in his field, he brought home a decent living. But as I saw it, that was the problem: Frank seldom worked in the field that he was skilled in. Most of the time he was preoccupied chasing after gold or oil. Frank endlessly and hopelessly chased pie in the sky. He eventually became discontented with his middle-class lifestyle. At times he reminded me of a spoiled prince who couldn't afford a crown. Through his scheming, he came to believe there was an easy way to acquire enormous wealth for his family. It was out there somewhere—he just had look under the right rock.

Soon he began turning his nose up at hourly wages or any form of labor. He used to poke fun at my pension for hard work. "You will never get anywhere working that hard, Jeff," he would say. "Oh well," he continued, "You'll make a wonderful employee for me one day." Sometimes he would disappear for months, leaving his wife and small children as he chased after treasure in faraway places.

Lonely and frustrated his wife said to us on one occasion, "My dear Frank is forever chasing rainbows in distant places. Sadly, when it is probably too late, he will one day realize the rainbow he has been searching for is in his own backyard!" Frank also had another problem—he was allergic to work, and avoided it like the plague. He reminded me of an ancient Arabian character named Al Hafed. The following is a paraphrasing of his story:

There lived not far from the River Indus an ancient Persian by the name of Al Hafed. Al Hafed owned a very large farm with orchards, grain fields, and gardens. He was a contented and wealthy man—contented because he was wealthy, and wealthy because he was contented. One day there visited this old farmer one of those ancient Buddhist priests, and he sat down by Al Hafed's fire and told that old farmer how this world of ours was made.

And then he declared that a diamond is the last and highest of God's mineral creations, as a woman is the last and highest of God's animal creations. The old priest told Al Hafed that if he had a handful of diamonds he could purchase a whole country, and with a mine of diamonds he could place his children upon thrones through the influence of their great wealth.

Al Hafed heard all about diamonds and how much they were worth, and went to bed that night a poor man—not that he had lost anything, but poor because he was discontented and discontented because he thought he was poor. He said: "I want a mine of diamonds!" So he lay awake all night, and early in the morning sought out the priest.

He awoke that priest out of his dreams and said to him, "Will you tell me where I can find diamonds?"

The priest said, "Diamonds? What do you want with diamonds?"

"I want to be immensely rich," said Al Hafed, "but I don't know where to go."

"Well," said the priest, "if you will find a river that runs over white sand between high mountains, in those sands you will always see diamonds."

"Do you really believe that there is such a river?"

"Plenty of them, plenty of them: all you have to do is just go and find them, then you have them."

Al Hafed said, "I will go." So he sold his farm, collected his money at interest, left his family in charge of a neighbor, and away he went in search of diamonds.

He went around into Palestine, then wandered on into Europe, and at last when his money was all spent and he was in rags, wretchedness, and poverty he stood on the shore of a bay in Barcelona, Spain. A tidal wave came rolling in through the Pillars of Hercules and the poor, afflicted, suffering man could not resist the awful temptation to cast himself into that incoming tide. He sank beneath its foaming crest, never to rise in this life again.

A few days after that, this same old priest who told Al Hafed how diamonds were made, came in to visit Al Hafed's successor, when he saw a flash of light on the mantel. He rushed up and said, "Here is a diamond—here is a diamond! Has Al Hafed returned?"

"No, no; Al Hafed has not returned and that is not a diamond; that is nothing but a stone; we found it right out here in our garden."

"But I know a diamond when I see it," said he. "That is a diamond!"

Then together they rushed to the garden and stirred up the white sands with their fingers and found other more beautiful, more valuable diamonds than the first.

If Al Hafed had remained at home and dug in his own cellar or in his own garden, instead of finding wretchedness, starvation, poverty, and death in a strange land, he would have had "acres of diamonds." For every acre, yes, every shovelful of that old farm afterwards revealed the gems which since have decorated the crowns of monarchs.[4]

What symbolic diamonds did Frank and Al Hafed surrender in their search for wealth? Both walked away from families; both believed the grass was greener and taller on the other side of the hill; both equated monetary wealth with speculation and discovery. And ironically, both walked away from productive jobs and hard work—key elements of success. Last but not least, both failed to recognize life's greatest treasures were hidden within their own hearts and within the humble walls of their own homes.

By the sweat of our brow we shall create our dreams. The riches of the world can be ours if we roll up our sleeves and attack life with some good, old-fashioned work. "Ideas must work through the brains and the arms of good and brave men, or they are no better than dreams."[5] Only you can bring your dream into physical being. How many masterpieces were envisioned but never created because paintbrushes were never lifted? We are told that even God toiled to bring the earth into physical being.

Therefore, the seventeenth amazing treasure reintroduces a revered, largely lost, ancient ritual that is chiefly credited for the advances of modern civilization. This treasure states:

"Work is the master word in ongoing life. It's the touchstone of progress, the measure of success, and the fount of hope."[6] *"The labor and sweat of our brows is so far from being a curse that without it our very bread would not be so great a blessing. If it were not for labor, men could neither eat so much, nor relish so pleasantly, nor sleep so soundly, nor be so healthful, so useful, so strong, so patient, so noble, nor so untempted."*[7]

Notes

1. John Ruskin, "Quotation Details," http://www.quotationspage.com/quote/2101.html
2. Dr. Tagore as quoted by Shahid Athar, "Spirituality, Medicine and Religion," http://islam-usa.com/ind200615.htm.
3. Howard W. Hunter, "Welfare Quotes by Subject," http://providentliving.org/content/display/0,11666,6481-1-3331-43,00.html.
4. Adapted from Russell H. Conwell, Robert Shackleton, Acres of Diamond: his life and achievements (New York: Harper & Sons, 1915).
5. Ralph Waldo Emerson "QuotationsBook," http://quotationsbook.com/quote/20078/.
6. Sir William Osler, as paraphrased by Spencer W. Kimball, "Family Preparedness," *Ensign*, May 1976, 124.

7. Jeremy Taylor, "Quotation Park: Labor," http://www.quotationpark.com/topics/labor.html.

"Things which matter most must never be at the mercy of things which matter least." —Goethe[1]

Amazing Treasure Number Eighteen

Honor: Holding Your Panache High!

After a stirring Sunday sermon, a son asked his father what he thought hell was like. His father thought for a moment and then responded, "Hell is one day meeting the man you could have been."

In September 1999, I suddenly became dizzy and developed a searing, debilitating headache. The pain was so great that I couldn't function. For several days I had a high fever. One night I felt something akin to a strong electrical current shooting from the back of my head down my spine. Days passed and the symptoms worsened. I felt certain I was dying.

Late one night, when I could stand the pain no longer, my wife rushed me to the hospital emergency room where I spent the night undergoing various tests. It seemed we had waited an eternity when I finally received a CAT scan. The doctor thought the symptoms sounded like a fast growing brain tumor, but tests were needed to be certain.

When I arrived in the room, I recognized the technician. This connection, and her beaming countenance, provided me some needed comfort. At the completion of the test, a doctor entered the glass room and, together with my friend, analyzed the pictures taken of my brain. Although I couldn't hear a word, I could tell by the expression on their faces that what they were seeing was not good.

When my friend re-entered the room, her expression had changed. After mustering the courage, I asked, "You found something didn't you?" Obviously uncomfortable, she explained that I would be pushed back to a cubical where the doctor and my wife would join me. There I would learn of my fate.

Oh, the lessons I learned during the next ten minutes. Fighting the thought every step of the way, I came in contact with that dreaded fate we call mortality. During these anxious and painful moments, I reflected on my life and how I desperately did not want it to end this way. "No! This cannot be," I told myself. My mind raced about uncontrollably. This was a nightmare and someone would awaken me soon; I endeavored to convince myself; but as hard as I tried to wish it away, I knew better. I was literally possessed with the thought that I was in no way prepared to die. "Please God," I uttered, "I have a vision of the kind of man I want to be when the end comes, and unfortunately, I am only a shadow of that individual." Like so many other men, I was a good father, but not the kind I had every intentions of one day becoming. Now I would be leaving very young children with only a memory of the reality . . . The weighty remorse was unbearable.

As never before, I pleaded with the Lord not to take me at this time. I promised to change my priorities if He would give me another opportunity. Images of my little family and my loved ones and friends flashed across my mind. I thought of how often I had sacrificed unnecessary time away from them for temporal pursuits. Unmasked by the imminence of death I realized, at least to some degree, that my heart belonged to the false and temporary treasures of earth. The alarming trivialness of these pursuits suddenly became clear and caused me deep and unbearable regret.

Several years later I am alive and well. Fortunately for me, God heard and answered my humble prayer and the long experience of pain and uncertainty helped purge and change my life forever. What the CAT scan revealed was an anomaly of sorts—not cancer. These words describe how I felt at hearing the news: "This is the beginning of a new day. God has given me this day to use as I will. I can waste it—or use it for good, but what I do today is important, because I am exchanging a day of my life for it! When tomorrow comes, this day will be gone forever, leaving in its place something that I have traded for it. I want it to be gain, and not loss; good and not evil; success, and not failure; in order that I shall not regret the price that I have paid for it."[2]

The all-consuming rat race of pursuing wealth can cheat us of reaching our spiritual potential. Knowing our time on earth is finite, we must choose wisely to ensure we get the most out of life and become the best we can be. Wisdom suggests we should create a prioritized list of hierarchical values to govern our lives. For example, we should embrace the gospel so completely that it penetrates every fiber of our being. It should be for us a cause that is larger than life. What is mere "purchase power" without such a cause?

"For what shall it profit a man, if he shall gain the whole world, and lose his own soul [in the process]?" (Mark 8:36). We must be careful not to neglect those things in life that are most precious to us. "For where your treasure is there will your heart be also" (Luke 12:34).

I have always been fascinated with the clever monkey trap. I am told it is nothing more than a box with a few small holes cut into the sides with large nuts placed in the bottom. When a monkey reaches in for a nut, his hand barely passes through the hole. But after he grabs a nut, he can't withdraw his hand. Caught, the monkey need only let go of the nut to save his life and go free. But few monkeys have the insight to let go of the lesser value in order to save the higher values. Thankfully, we are not all monkeys.

How many of us constantly exchange freedom and life for nuts? Too many of us are not skilled at identifying these values. We need to sit down, prioritize, record, and give our goals a place of prominence in our lives. We need to define the path that leads to our goals. Above all, we need to know what to cling to and what to let go. In this crazy world of mixed up priorities, how are we to know the nuts from eternal things? In the Book of Mormon, we find Lehi's telling dream of the tree of life, which depicts you, me, and others clinging to the iron rod (word of the Lord) and being chided by the multitudes in the large and spacious building (pride of the world). Because of shame or pride, many of us let go and wander down forbidden paths. The story is a gripping analogy of today's world.

In the movie *Cyrano de Bergerac*, a stiff upper-class gentleman named Conte De Guiche speaks of his enemy, Cyrano, in this way, "He knew no [false] allegiance, a free man in thought and deed. I know I have everything, he nothing, but gladly I would shake his hand. Sometimes I envy him. When your life has been a success . . . without making any real stand, you feel a slight disgust within, but no real remorse—just a faint discomfort. The decal robes of fur sweep up the stairs of state with lost illusions and regret." (In the battle of Arras against the Spaniards, de Guiche dropped the scarf, or panache, which signified he was an army captain, in order to escape death—something Cyrano would never have done.)

The panache is our crowning jewel. It is the culmination of what our life represents. Each of us should stand for something, and like Cyrano, be willing to sacrifice all to uphold those beliefs. Unlike de Guiche, Cyrano was a man of principle. At the conclusion of his life, Cyrano did not leave behind a legacy of regret and mediocrity. Even his enemy envied him. Cyrano's beliefs were a way of life, not a decorated scarf to be quickly discarded when things heated up, got dangerous, or unpopular.[3]

Peter and John were offered money for their "panache."

> Now when the apostles which were at Jerusalem heard that Samaria had received the word of God, they sent unto them Peter and John: Who, when they were come down, prayed for them, that they might receive the Holy Ghost: (For as yet he was fallen upon none of them: only they were baptized in the name of the Lord Jesus.) Then laid they their hands on them, and they received the Holy Ghost. And when Simon saw that through the laying on of the apostles' hands the Holy Ghost was given, he offered them money, Saying, Give me also this power, that on whomsoever I lay hands, he may receive the Holy Ghost. But Peter said unto him, Thy money perish with thee, because thou hast thought that the gift of God may be purchased with money. . . . Repent therefore of this thy wickedness, and pray God, if perhaps the thought of thine heart may be forgiven thee (Acts 8:14–20, 22).

Mother Teresa saw human suffering and dedicated her life to bringing relief. Through her compassion and conviction, she caught the attention of mighty nations, which followed her lead. One voice in the darkness made a difference for countless thousands.

We must refuse to surrender our birthright for pottage! Throughout our marriage, my wife and I had a long-standing dream of owning a little farm in a beautiful mountain valley. Several years ago we found nine acres for sale near Kamas, Utah. It was everything we had dreamed. On the south border, a small brook complimented the lush green pasture as it meandered through the cottonwoods. I vividly remember walking around the property for the first time and feeling magic I hadn't experienced since my childhood at Christmas time. It was breathtaking. A wild, sweet scent was carried down the valley by a gentle breeze from the high Uintah Mountains. Everything felt so right; it was perfect. We decided to make it ours and called the owners that evening.

During the conversation with the owners, we learned the acreage was landlocked. The county would not grant a permit to build a home on this property unless frontage along the main road was acquired. The land would be no more than expensive horse property.

I spent hours traveling to the County Seat in Coalville, where I poured over land plats and consulted with County planners and engineers. During this time my father found a buyer for his farm in Marion and wanted to know if I wanted ten acres. Because acquiring the nine acres was still uncertain, I called the owner and explained my predicament. Although we had nothing recorded on paper, he gave me his word and reassured me the property would be ours as soon as I could solve the problem. He promised me several times that he wouldn't sell it out from underneath us. I therefore reluctantly called my father and turned him down on a choice piece of my grandfather's farm. It pained me to let it go, but that's how badly we wanted the nine acres.

Thereafter, I dutifully called every owner with property adjacent to the nine-acres. Finally, one of them agreed to sell me a sliver of his property located between the main road and the landlocked parcel. Of course he wanted a handsome price. Nonetheless, we had found a way and the county planners eventually approved it.

As soon as I could get in touch with the owner, I explained I had found a way to free up the property. "We sold the property last week," was his stoic reply.

You guessed it. The property owner who had agreed to sell me the necessary sliver of land liked my idea, and on the sly presented an alternative offer. Years of work and dreams ended abruptly. It was a double blow for us. We lost both the nine acres and a chance for a piece of my grandparents' farm.

To say the least, we were very disappointed. The landowner compromised his honor for expedient money. He dropped his panache in the mud when dollars were flashed. Although I have forgiven him, I wonder if he feels de Guiche's faint discomfort and slight disgust within. To be truly happy, we must protect against compromising our honor.

A few years later, I was in the market for a small tractor to compliment the little farm we purchased in Riverton, Utah. Have you ever tried to buy a small tractor? For the number of tractors available, there is a high demand. However, early one Saturday morning I was looking through the classifieds and I happened on a John Deere tractor with a front-end loader and several implements priced within my range at nine thousand dollars. I wasted no time, jumped in my car, and traveled to the residence in Murray. As I waited for the door to open, a beautiful Ford truck pulled along the curb in front of the house. It was another customer. An elderly gentleman answered the door, and I asked him about the tractor. He took me into the field where it was parked. It was exactly what I had been looking for, so I asked him if he would accept eight thousand dollars. He smiled and said his phone had been ringing off the hook with people making appointments and felt certain he could get what he was asking. Having looked for months, I knew this was true.

The power-stroke diesel truck idling at the curb served as a reminder another customer was waiting after I finished. Suddenly, I had the sick realization I only had ten dollars in my wallet. I explained my predicament to the old farmer and jokingly offered him the ten dollars if he would hold it for a few hours until I could bring him a more realistic down payment. He smiled and said, "Young man, I don't need your money. Your word of honor is worth a great deal more and will be plenty sufficient." We shook hands, and off I went to the credit union. When I returned, the truck was still parked in front of the house. My heart dropped and I thought of the nine acres we had missed out on recently. I ran to the door and knocked. The gentleman answered the door chuckling and said, "This appears to be your lucky day. My phone has never stopped ringing with requests and offers about the tractor, and the man in the truck has offered me cash on the spot with a handsome bonus if I would forget about you."

This man's honor was not for sale. He saved the tractor for me based upon a handshake and promise to return. He even threw in a new one hundred twenty dollar battery before I picked up the tractor a few days later.

This kind old farmer renewed my dwindling hope in mankind. His panache was not for sale at any price. He was a man of honor and it showed in his eyes, the window to his heart. Like Cyrano, the honorable, old farmer would not drop his panache for advancement, money, or position. He also drew a line in the sand, stood his ground, and held his panache about him tightly.

As I turned eighteen and neared my lifelong dream to serve the Lord on a full-time mission, many new temptations were suddenly laid before me. I discovered girls—or maybe girls discovered me—and I discovered fast and fancy cars. A distant neighbor had one of the coolest and fastest cars in the neighborhood—a hopped-up, candy apple red, S.S. Chevy Chevelle. Even though he chose not to serve the Lord on a mission, in my limited view Gary still had everything that was important. He enjoyed a well-paying job, and pretty girls lined up to date and be seen with him. What more could any young man want, right? Well, thanks to a whole lot of coaching and direction from my parents, as much as I wanted to at the time, I didn't follow in my idol's footsteps. Instead, exercising faith, I cut my hair, bought a dozen stiff white shirts, and four ill-fitting suits; three pairs of mailman-style shoes, a new pair of scriptures, and then said good-bye to the girls and family and headed to the Missionary Training Center in Provo, Utah. It only took a few months into my mission when I found myself looking for a quiet corner in which to fall on my knees and thank the Lord for my mission and for the eternal things I was learning and doing there. With tears of joy and gratitude, families and individuals we were teaching and baptizing were seeking me out to thank me from the bottom of their hearts for choosing to serve a mission.

After serving the Lord for two years, I returned to my hometown to find certain things had changed. My little brothers and sisters had changed. Many of the girls I had dated were now married. I had no money in the bank. But everyone said it was me who had changed the most.

Tragically, Gary had been forced to get married. His lifeless Chevelle was now sitting in a far corner of his parents' yard on blocks, its once brilliant color now oxidized. The chrome wheels were rusting; the fancy tires and diamond-tucked leather interior were sun-baked and rotting. Rust spots bubbled along the seams and wheel wells. This once alluring, earthly treasure that had been the object of so much coveting among my peers that had brought its owner so much satisfaction and recognition, was now an eyesore—slowly decaying. "Lay not up for yourselves treasures upon earth, where moth and rust doth corrupt, and where thieves break through and steal: But lay up for yourselves treasures in heaven, where neither moth nor rust doth corrupt, and where thieves do not break through nor steal" (Matthew 6:19–20).

Eternal value must be recognized and pursued at the expense of monetary values. Many years ago, I met a young lady named Pamela Woodruff. I saw something in her that was rare and unique. She was as beautiful on the inside as she was on the outside. When in her presence I felt I could accomplish anything. In her I saw unearthly value.

Because I believe marriage is the single greatest decision to be made in this life, it is at the top of my hierarchical values. As a result, I dropped as many of my worldly pursuits as possible and pursued her with great determination. Today, she is my wife and answers to the name of Pamela Hair. For both my children and me, no finer value exists. She is the center and heart of our home. I shudder to think where I would be if I hadn't been willing to sacrifice material values to pursue her. The well-known Christmas story of Ebenezer Scrooge so clearly demonstrates what happens to a life that places money over relationships and principles, and none of us wants to go there![4]

While camping recently, my family discovered an ancient Indian petroglyph on a high mountain cliff. Such an unexpected find was truly awe-inspiring. We marveled at the size, intricacy, and detail of the painting, and how it had endured through the centuries. Although the artist and his people had ceased to exist hundreds of years ago, the art had transcended time and spoken to and influenced many generations. As we stood there on what seemed to be sacred ground studying an ancient peoples' handiwork, I asked my children to ponder what aspect of their personal lives they wished to pass on to future generations. The answers were both profound and reflective. Love, friendship, and honor were among the responses.

We would do well to ask ourselves, "In my comings and goings, what has my life and name come to represent among those who know me best? Is it consistent with my higher values?" If not, heaven has given you a few precious moments to change.

As the sun rises and sets, let us prioritize our values and keep the eternal ones. We must hold these values high above the magnetic allure and sophistry of this world and interweave them into the fabric of our lives. This will give us strength of character and set us apart from the ordinary. Aligning ourselves with eternal principles transforms our lives from pointless struggling to valiant and meaningful purposes.

Hence, a light that will never dim in the darkest of nights, the eighteenth amazing treasure is as a brilliant supernova. It proclaims:

"A man is already of consequence in the world when it is known that he can be relied on, that when he says he knows a thing, he does know it—that when he says he will do a thing, he can do, and does it."[5] *As Cyrano said, "My old enemies are falsehood, cowardice, and compromise—I'll fight one and all. That these enemies would take everything—except the one thing I would keep in spite of them, my panache."*[6]

Notes

1. "Johann von Goethe Quotes," http://www.quotes.net/quote/1138.
2. Heartsill Wilson "A New Day," http://www.affirmations-for-success.com/success-poem.html.
3. *Cyrano de Bergerac*, DVD, directed by Jean-Paul Rappeneau, (1990, Hollywood: MGM, 2004).
4. Charles Dickens, *A Christmas Carol* (London: Bradbury & Evans, 1858).
5. Samuel Smiles, *Character* (Chicago: Belford, Clarke & Co., 1881).
6. *Cyrano de Bergerac*, DVD.

"O Goddess Earth, O all-enduring wide expanses! Salutation to thee. Now I am going to begin cultivation. Be pleased, O virtuous one."
—Ancient Sanskrit prayer[1]

Amazing Treasure Number Nineteen

Health: And the Gods Planted a Garden (Abraham 5:8)

Carefully negotiating the strands of barbed wire, I climbed through the fence and made my way toward the abandoned tractor. His brilliant green had dulled and rusted from years of exposure and neglect. Wires dangled about the once powerful engine. Its tires were weathered and rotting, the rims had partially sunk into the ground under its heavy mass.

As a boy I dreamed of living on a farm in a quaint little town. I wanted this dream so badly at times, I swear I could smell the scent of homemade breads and pies wafting in the country breeze as they cooled in my mother's window. Isn't it strange where life takes you? In contrast, I have lived the balance of my life in a bustling city with paved highways and jutting walls of concrete and steel. The nearest I came to living my dream was the summer stints on my grandmother's dilapidated farm a few weeks each year. On long summer days, in this high mountain valley, my younger brother and I would play on old tractors and chase cows through lush, waist-high grass.

As a child, more than anything else, I wanted a tractor. It is symbolic of things that are good and wholesome; strong and powerful, yet simple and unpretentious. What intrigues me most about the tractor is what it makes possible. When pitted against the rocky, sunbaked earth, the tractor hunkers down, its huge treaded tires turn, digging in, black smoke belches out the stack, while beneath it the earth crumbles under sheer torque and power—yielding up the treasure of life and health of humanity and all living creatures—soil. Ezra Taft Benson taught, "There are blessings in being close to the soil, in raising your own food even if it is only a garden in your yard and a fruit tree or two."[2]

As William Butler Yeats put it thus, "All that we did, all that we said or sang must come from contact with the soil."[3] In this modern, advanced age of enlightenment where preventable illnesses and diseases are now inflicting children, my powerful message is simple: move away from nutritiously bankrupt foods that are processed in factories and return to one of the ideals of my childhood dream—the family garden. "To dig in one's own earth, with one's own space, does life hold anything better?"[4] The voice of the Lord has recently declared:

> And again, verily I say unto you, all wholesome herbs God hath ordained for the constitution, nature, and use of man. Every herb in the season thereof, and every fruit in the season thereof; all these to be used with prudence and thanksgiving. Yea, flesh also of beasts and of the fowls of the air, I, the Lord, have ordained for the use of man with thanksgiving; nevertheless they are to be used sparingly. . . . All grain is ordained for the use of man and of beasts, to be the staff of life, not only for man but for the beasts of the field, and the fowls of heaven, and all wild animals that run or creep on the earth. . . . All grain is good for the food of man . . . as also the fruit of the vine; that which yieldeth fruit, whether in the ground or above the ground (D&C 89:10–12, 14, 16).

As already mentioned, in 1999, I lost a balance in my life. I did this by writing checks my body could not cash. In addition to working an average twelve-hour day, my work environment became more hard-hitting and stressful. Atop an already high-pressure vocation, I got a boss who decided to be difficult. I was running and exercising two or three hours a day, five days a week. Additionally, I was in school and pulling a heavy load. My life was busy; yet apparently not busy enough. Did I mention I was the acting general contractor on a house I was building for my family in Riverton, Utah. I wish to emphasize the word "acting" because building a house was not in the repertoire of things I knew how to do. But in my enthusiasm this was a minor obstacle because I could learn these skills while building the house, right? Too often I have been the duck-your-head-and-plow-forward type who sometimes unintentionally walks where angels fear to tread. Many were the nights I would retire to the camper on the building site at one or two in the morning. The next day I would arise just to start the marathon all over again.

This year and these battles were to be very different from those I had experienced previously. For the first time in my life, I was not eating right. Nutritionally speaking I was burning up considerably more than I was depositing. My wife and kids were staying in a home two hours away and eating turned out to be more of an afterthought in my daily grind and usually it came out of a can. It progressed to the point that nothing sat well with me. After months of working like a crazed maniac, I found my "can do" attitude began to fail me; for no apparent reason, my confidence took a dive. More and more, I would find myself easily overwhelmed, indecisive, and irritated. I found to get anything done I had to constantly push myself as I tired easily and wanted to sit all the time. Concentrating was next to impossible.

Despite the fact that my body was desperately trying to tell me something, I was busy cracking the whip and pushed forward with greater zeal. At times I found myself falling asleep or spacing out the very moment I sat down. Before long I developed a nagging dizziness and frontal headache. I tried my usual remedies in an effort to kick it, including a visit to the ophthalmologist, doctor, and dentist. The doctor eventually put me on a regiment of antibiotics believing I probably had a sinus infection. With no results, he put me on a second, more powerful, antibiotic. To my dismay this worsened my condition.

In the main, I had work that needed to be done. I therefore decided to counter this harassing development and began to exercise harder and longer. My logic was to strengthen my body's immunity. Work pressures continued to heat up and regardless of my efforts, there was no solution in the horizon. Now, even more checks were written on an already overdrawn account. As I look back in hindsight, I feel foolish. I clearly see that I was a ticking time bomb. After a return trip from Boise, Idaho, my condition deteriorated, and I developed a strange electrical current that ran up and down my spine. By this time my headache was near blinding. My head was literally so hot, it was uncomfortable to the touch and was sweating profusely. In a near panic my wife rushed me to the hospital emergency room. The pain was so unbearable, I was relieved to finally be under the care of medical professionals.

Over the next few months, I found this was indeed a false sense of security. I was much worse for the wear when the doctors finished experimenting with me. Besides nearly snuffing out my fledging pilot light, I learned even in this modern age of enlightenment there is much about the body they do not understand; and the practice of medicine can be just that: a hit and miss practice. Though they gave it a valiant effort, a few weeks before Christmas the doctors admitted they were completely baffled, and there was currently nothing more they could do for me. We were told my situation would need to deteriorate further before a proper diagnosis could be made. My doctor wondered if it was the beginning stages of multiple sclerosis.

With the medical experts baffled, my dear wife found herself alone with a difficult patient and a young family in peril. Instinctively, she packed and moved us to our little home in the country. Here, she effectively isolated me from the stresses that were contributing to my condition. She painstakingly prepared herbal teas and nutritious meals. It was here I daily contemplated the call from my friend that eventually changed my fatalistic attitude. It was acting upon his words, and the encouragement of my wife, that gave me the strength to get out of bed, dress warmly, and go for daily walks.

It was on a long, lonely stretch of dirt road where I desperately pleaded with the Lord with all the energy of my heart, to either heal or take me. In the end, it appeared my days were still numbered.

Hippocrates said, "Let food be thy medicine and medicine be thy food."[5] Sometime ago I had an older friend who developed an internal infection that became life threatening. He developed a high fever and shortness of breath. Gains from the efforts of the doctors proved only temporary. As his condition worsened, he fell out of life and was reduced to the couch or bed. To keep his fever down, the doctors had him on a strong steroid, and the strength had to be continually increased as the weeks passed in order to achieve the same results. Each time an attempt was made to wean him off the steroids, his fever would return with a vengeance. In addition, the doctor had him on a strong antibiotic regimen. One day I stopped for a visit. I felt moved to talk with this couple about their nutritional habits and daily diet. I learned they were drinking soda instead of water. I learned they were practically eating out daily. When they could not grab a taco or hamburger at a fast food joint, they heated up frozen dinners in the microwave. I also learned he had been under prolonged stress.

The body is made up of mostly water and the liberal intake of this most precious commodity is essential. Among a myriad of things, the proper intake of water cleanses the body of waste. And a clean blood supply and properly hydrated organs and tissues are essential for long-term health. One of the executives I rubbed shoulders with challenged me to never pass by a drinking fountain without taking a drink. I challenged my friend to drink several cups of water daily. He accepted.

As suggested by the Lord in section 89 of the Doctrine and Covenants, vegetables and fruits are good for man. Although we may never know all the reasons, who can argue with the wisdom of our body's creator? Sometimes we must obey in faith because we believe in the voice of the Lord. This much we do know: In addition to providing the body with essential minerals and vitamins, vegetables and fruits are loaded with disease fighting phytochemicals. Recently, ten thousand varieties have been documented. Modern research has linked these ten thousand, stripling little guys with potent disease fighting capabilities. This is why growing a garden is so fundamentally critical; because fruit can be picked directly from the vine, fresh, with little, if any, of its natural potency lost through packaging, shipping, and long durations in storage. A garden will get us off the couch and out into the fresh air, moving. A cardinal rule to remember about gardening, however, is that no plant is better than the soil it is grown in. If the soil is deficient, the plant will have similar deficiencies. Hence, learn and engage yourself in the wonderful art of composting. I challenged my friend and his wife to prepare and eat the fresh vegetables and fruits I volunteered from my highly composted, organic garden. Under the gun and out of sheer desperation, they accepted.

Emotionally, my friend was a wreck as well. Like me, he too was convinced he was dying and cycled this information over and over in his mind. I recounted for them the smile-for-no-reason story and challenged him to have faith in his priesthood blessings. I challenged him to change his self-dialogue to thinking more positively, even though he would not feel like it. I challenged him to dwell on the good things in his life. And again, he promised to try.

Before I left I warned my friend not to expect things to happen too quickly. I explained it took him many years to get into this predicament, and it would probably take a good while to get out. Even I was not prepared for the miracle that followed. Within several weeks of this regiment, my friend was off the harsh steroid and back to living life to its fullest. "And there were some who died with fevers, which at some seasons of the year were very frequent in the land—but not so much so with fevers, because of the excellent qualities of the many plants and roots which God had prepared to remove the cause of diseases" (Alma 46:40).

In retrospect, I believe it was those three things that eventually healed me: first, isolation from the offending stresses; second, the consumption of nutritional foods and water; and finally, personal prayer and priesthood blessings.

Although doctors play an important role and have a place in society, we cannot in good faith relinquish the responsibility of our health to them or anyone else. As popular as they are today, pharmaceutical drugs will never be a healthy substitute for proper nutrition and exercise. Spoonful after spoonful, many of us are foolishly eating our way toward disease and broken health. Let us repent of this neglect and obey the word of the Lord by eating whole grains and fresh foods from our own gardens. Spencer W. Kimball taught: "Grow all the food that you possibly can on your own property, if water is available, berry bushes, grapevines, fruit trees are most desirable. Plant them if your climate is right for their growth. Grow vegetables and eat those grown in your own yard. Even those residing in apartments or condominiums can generally grow a little food in pots and planters."[7]

Sometime before his astonishing interpretation of King Nebuchadnezzar's dream, Daniel had already made an unusual name for himself by refusing to defile himself with the King's wine and meat. Instead, he requested to eat pulse (plant seed and legumes). The prince of the eunuchs worried Daniel and his few followers would not have the physical prowess of the others who were eating the King's rich foods and wine, thereby offending him and possibly drawing his lethal wrath upon them. But Daniel persisted and proposed a ten-day showdown between the two diets to which the prince reluctantly agreed. At the end of ten days, the results were miraculous! Daniel and his fellows were not only in better shape physically, but mentally as well. "And in all matters of wisdom and understanding, that the king enquired of them, he found them ten times better than all the magicians and astrologers that were in all his realm" (Daniel 1:20).

Good health is not something we accidentally fall into as we age, and it is more involved than the occasional lip service it characteristically gets. Rather we must actively and aggressively extend ourselves to assure its continuation and protection. If you are fortunate enough to have good health, you will seldom have cause to think about it; but if you lose it, I promise you will think of little else.

Good health involves more than abstinence from the obvious. Concerning this God-given stewardship Joseph Smith taught that "it is the will of God that man should repent and serve him in health, and in the strength and power of his mind, in order to secure his blessings."[8] Good health enhances any financial situation, but bad health can easily destroy the happiness of this world's most wealthy.

Sown from the fertile star fields of perpetuity, the nineteenth amazing treasure offers the humble seeker this truth:

The blessing of a long and fruitful life requires living close to the soil by cultivating a garden. As much as possible, our sustenance should be food in its most natural form, fruits and vegetables from the vine and whole grains. Last but not least, liberally drink the cleansing health liquid of earth—water. Beyond question, one of the greatest treasures is our health. It too is worth the wealth of earth. For if we obey these sayings, we shall not only live, but we shall live well!

Today, each breath I take is a wonderful blessing—not one can be taken for granted. Sometimes I just sit in a quiet corner and listen to my body take in fresh air and then expel it. My body does it on its own without any conscious effort from me—what a marvelous little miracle! It was not always true. Have you ever lost your health? I did. So count your blessings. With health you are among the wealthiest and possibly the happiest people alive.

Notes

1. "Sanskrit prayer," http://www.digdug.cx/earth/3.html.
2. Ezra Taft Benson, "Prepare for the Days of Tribulation," *Ensign*, Nov. 1980, 32.
3. "Yeats Quote," http://www.enotes.com/famous-quotes/all-that-we-did-all-that-we-said-or-sangmust-come.
4. Beverly Nichols, "Quotes," http://www.gardendigest.com/earth.htm.
5. Hippocrates, "Goodreads," http://www.goodreads.com/quotes/show/62262.
6. Richard Béliveau and Denis Gingras, *Foods to Fight Cancer* (New York: DK Publishing, 2007).
7. Spencer W. Kimball, "The True Way of Life and Salvation," *Ensign*, May 1978, 4.
8. Joseph Smith, *Teachings of the Presidents of the Church: Joseph Smith* (Salt Lake City: Intellectual Reserve, 2007), 197.

"I can be too old for so many things like begging for candy and jumping on big trampolines but there is one thing I am never too old for . . . spending time with my dad and not much more."
—Nine-year-old Mariah Lin Hair

Amazing Treasure Number Twenty

Children: The Heritage of the Lord

The impact choices have on us is openly revealed in the life of the prospector who dutifully worked his gold mine. His work ethic was above reproach and the envy of those who knew him. The harder he applied himself, the more distant his fame spread upon the land. As his treasure grew, many called him great. People near and far clamored to associate with him and expended great effort to be numbered among his friends. Finally, with the better part of his life spent and the last of the gold stacked upon the wagon, he hitched the team of mules up and headed into town. With the hard labor behind him and with his wealth in tow, he would live as a king for the remainder of his days.

While attentive clerks unloaded the heavy bags into the huge bank vault, the manager indiscriminately opened a bag and closely examined a single nugget he found therein. After studying the stone for a few seconds, the expert turned to the spent, old man and said, "I'm terribly sorry, sir, but what you have here is nothing more than worthless pyrite ore, more commonly referred to as fool's gold." Tragically, in his zeal and ignorance, the hard-working prospector had foolishly spent his life pursuing the wrong thing. Imagine the grief he could have spared himself if he had sought the advice of the expert from the beginning instead of waiting until the end.

The only signs of life on the barren mountainside were juniper trees, sagebrush, and a lone jackrabbit that darted in and out of the aged, weathered tombstones. My daughters and I were standing in the cemetery of the once legendary town of Frisco, Utah, located at the base of the great Horn Silver Mine. In its heyday the "Horn" was said to be the most lucrative silver mine in the entire country. Prospectors and laborers from all walks of life were drawn to the monetary potential of this wild and untamed town. Saloons and brothels lined Main Street and killings and lawlessness were rampant.

Today, the wind howls relentlessly and the shifting sand slowly but continuously erodes what little remains of the dreams and structures erected by these people. A sense of misplaced ambitions struck me as I surveyed the utter desolation. Standing there at the foot of a little grave, in the most unlikely of places, I experienced a personal paradigm shift. It hit me like never before—children are the true wealth of earth. Furthermore, I felt an odd connection with the parents of this child. Sadly, sometimes it's necessary to lose something before we understand its true value. A hard lump settled in my throat with my young, living daughters standing nearby. I instinctively knew of the parent's loss and devastation. Together, my daughters and I read the dust-covered words inscribed on stone from this grieving couple. "Tis a little grave but oh have care for worldwide hopes are buried here. . . . How much of light, how much of joy is buried with my darling boy."

Poet Charles M. Dickinson once wrote,

> They are idols of hearts and of households;
> They are angels of God in disguise;
> His sunlight still sleeps in their tresses,
> His glory still gleams in their eyes;
> These truants from home and from heaven,
> They have made me more manly and mild;
> And I know now how Jesus could liken
> The kingdom of God to a child.[1]

Notwithstanding, "In the beginning was the Word, and the Word was with God, and the Word was God. The same was in the beginning with God. All things were made by him and without him was not anything made that was made. . . . And the Word was made flesh, and dwelt among us, and we beheld his glory, the glory as of the only begotten of the Father, full of grace and truth" (John 1:1–3, 14). Thus, Jehovah the mighty God of the Old Testament, of Abraham, Isaac, and Jacob, of Moses and of

Noah, was made flesh and in accordance with heavenly messengers was named Jesus. With poetic jubilation, Isaiah exclaimed, "For unto us a child is born, unto us a son is given: and the government shall be upon his shoulder: and his name shall be called Wonderful, Counselor, The mighty God, The everlasting Father, The Prince of Peace" (Isaiah 9:6).

Truth is indeed stranger than fiction, for this reality even surpasses the wildest known mystical legends of human imagination. What insight could we gleam from such a being of this stature whose words are heaven's obligation? Would the insight of this master expert be of eternal worth to you and me as we make our way through this world of many voices? Although worth little in worldly terms, Mark recorded that "they brought young children to him, that he should touch them: and his disciples rebuked those that brought them. But when Jesus saw it, he was much displeased, and said unto them, Suffer the little children to come unto me, and forbid them not: for such is the kingdom of God" (Mark 10:13–14).

Even at this stage in His ministry, it appears His disciples had missed the mark and were entirely clueless concerning the importance Jesus placed on children. In this stern rebuke from the Master, He makes it very clear that children are not to be trifled with. They are in fact, the populace of heaven—the crowning jewel of mankind. So heavenlike are these little creatures that we are told in order to gain entrance to heaven's gate, we must become like them. Few events adequately capture the Lord's love for children as does the scriptural account of His visit to the ancient American Nephites, shortly after His resurrection.

> And he took their little children, one by one, and blessed them, and prayed unto the Father for them. And when he had done this he wept again; and he spake unto the multitude, and said unto them: Behold your little ones. And as they looked to behold they cast their eyes towards heaven, and they saw the heavens open, and they saw angels descending out of heaven as it were in the midst of fire; and they came down and encircled those little ones about, and they were encircled about with fire; and the angels did minister unto them. And the multitude did see and hear and bear record; and they know that their record is true for they all of them did see and hear, every man for himself. (3 Nephi 17:21–24)

There is no doubt that for years to follow these twenty-five hundred Nephites did indeed "behold their little ones." In fact, they looked upon their children with an entirely new awakening following this supernal event. How could they not? Before their eyes stood the prophesied Christ who had descended from the heavens after unprecedented tempests earthquakes, upheavals, fires, whirlwinds, and three days of darkness. In the backdrop of this riveted undivided attention, Jesus tenderly stretched forth His hands and blessed the children one by one, and as He did He wept. To seal His deeds with an exclamation, angels enshrouded in fire fell from the heavens to encircle, not Him, but their little ones (3 Nephi 17:21–24). So moved were the multitude that they diligently turned their hearts and attention to their children and loved and taught them, insomuch that there followed over two hundred years of peace and righteousness throughout the land.

In another strongly worded warning, Jesus said, "But whoso shall offend one of these little ones which believe in me, it were better for him that a millstone were hanged about his neck and that he were drowned in the depth of the sea" (Matthew 18:6). The offense spoken of here can come about in many ways. Beyond question the children of the world are neglected and under attack. The family, which is responsible for providing children a solid foundation of love, nurturing, and instruction, is under siege. Edward Gibbon in 1776–1788 set forth in his famous book *Decline and Fall of the Roman Empire* the reasons he believed Rome fell. One of these was the "undermining of the dignity and sanctity of the home which is the basis for human society."[2] History is replete with great societies that failed due to the deterioration of the home.

Elder M. Russell Ballard stated: "From a diabolically tactical point of view, fighting the family makes sense to Satan. When he wants to disrupt the work of the Lord, he doesn't poison the world's peanut butter supply, thus bringing the Church's missionary system to its collective knees. He doesn't send a plague of laryngitis to afflict the Mormon Tabernacle Choir. . . . When evil wants to strike out and disrupt the essence of God's work, it attacks the family."[3] Too many parents have allowed themselves to become diverted, chasing after fool's gold. With parents thus preoccupied, the home has been left defenseless to the raised sword of our sworn enemy. When parents are preoccupied, societies crumble and nations fall. Isaiah's watch cry is haunting, "Watchman what of the night? Watchman what of the night?" (Isaiah 21:11).

Approximately two thousand years later, this same Jesus, now glorified, resurrected, and with the title of Savior bestowed upon Him, in complete harmony with previous messages, issued a stern rebuke to the young prophet of the restoration as well as a few other prominent Church leaders. "You have not taught your children light and truth, according to the commandments; and that wicked one hath power, as yet, over you, and this is the cause of your affliction. And now a commandment I give unto you,—if you will be delivered you shall set in order your own house, for there are many things that are not right in your house. . . . Your family must needs repent and forsake some things, and give more earnest heed unto your sayings, or be removed out of their place" (D&C 93:42–43, 48).

With the myriad of things He could have counseled them about, and with the restoration of the gospel still in its infancy, what essential deficiency was the Lord most concerned with that these prominent leaders shared in common? What might the Lord say to us about the current status of our homes? Do we expend our time and energies pursuing the things of this world at the expense of our children? Perhaps this too is the cause of our affliction. Like the shortsighted miner, it should be remembered that a few seconds of instruction from the expert exposed counterfeit treasure from the authentic article.

As Phillips Brooks put it, "Oh, that there could thrill through the being of our young [people] some electrical sense that they are God's [children], that they might . . . live the life and attain the nature which are rightly theirs."[4]

God through His prophets has recently given us a divine charter to guide seeking parents and ensure the effectiveness and survival of the family. Because of all the misleading and cunning influences of our time a voice of truth is urgently needed. For "out of all this awful and aching battle of blinding lights, without one shadow to give shape to them, we must manage somehow to trace and to track a star."[5] The Family Proclamation is such a star.[6]

Mothers, you must be ever cautious in abdicating the care and development of your children to others or to the institutions of man. Lasting peace and happiness are to be found in fostering children. You will "have no greater joy than to hear that [your] children walk in truth" (3 John 1:4). In the wide scale absence of mothers from the home, there is no adequate surrogate. Without the daily, moment to moment imparting of her values, with the absence of her gentle, nurturing disposition and guiding hand "iniquity shall abound, [and] the love of many shall wax cold" (Matthew 24:12).

As a child, I remember my father extolling my mother's many virtues. On one particular occasion, he taught his young children about her unselfish nature. Among other things, he explained that our mother hadn't purchased a new coat for herself in many years so that we could be properly dressed.

Mothers, these are among your divine attributes, which have helped shape, develop, and strengthen mankind. I am your son, and we are your children and no matter where we go or who we become, in our mind's eye you will go before us. Your life and imparted wisdom will serve as our moral compass through long and difficult years. Due to your optimism, we will find happiness amongst peril and confusion. Because of your imparted values, we are not soft, but steadfast. Thanks to you, mother, we know who we are and we will make a stand.

Stephen L. Richards, quoted from an article, written by a veteran criminal court judge, entitled "Nine Words That Can Stop Juvenile Delinquency." The nine words suggested by the judge were "Put father back at the head of the family."[7]

Fathers, are we "ever learning, and never able to come to the knowledge of the truth?" (2 Timothy 3:7). Have we busied ourselves with unnecessary goals, cares, or pleasures? Often in our self-inflicted diversions, the treasure chest has become more important than the precious jewels inside. The following story illustrates this beautifully.

> Listen, son: I am saying this as you lie asleep, one little paw crumpled under your cheek and the blond curls stickily wet on your damp forehead. I have stolen into your room alone. Just a few minutes ago, as I sat reading my paper in the library, a stifling wave of remorse swept over me. Guiltily I came to your bedside.
>
> There are the things I was thinking, son: I had been cross to you. I scolded you as you were dressing for school because you gave your face merely a dab with a towel. I took you to task for not cleaning your shoes. I called out angrily when you threw some of your things on the floor.
>
> At breakfast I found fault, too. You spilled things. You gulped down your food. You put your elbows on the table. You spread butter too thick on your bread. And as you started off to play and I made for my train, you turned and waved a hand and called, "Good-bye, Daddy!" and I frowned, and said in reply, "Hold your shoulders back!"
>
> Then it began all over again in the late afternoon. As I came up

the road I spied you, down on your knees, playing marbles. There were holes in your stockings. I humiliated you before your boyfriends by marching you ahead of me to the house. Stockings were expensive—and if you had to buy them you would be more careful! Imagine that, son, from a father!

Do you remember, later, when I was reading in the library, how you came in timidly, with a sort of hurt look in your eyes? When I glanced up over my paper, impatient at the interruption, you hesitated at the door "What is it you want?" I snapped.

You said nothing, but ran across in one tempestuous plunge, and threw your arms around my neck and kissed me, and your small arms tightened with an affection that God had set blooming in your heart and which even neglect could not wither. And then you were gone, pattering up the stairs. Well, son, it was shortly afterwards that my paper slipped from my hands and a terrible sickening fear came over me. What has habit been doing to me? The habit of finding fault, of reprimanding—this was my reward to you for being a boy. It was not that I did not love you; it was that I expected too much of youth. I was measuring you by the yardstick of my own years.

And there was so much that was good and fine and true in your character. The little heart of you was as big as the dawn itself over the wide hills. This was shown by your spontaneous impulse to rush in and kiss me good night. Nothing else matters tonight, son. I have come to your bedside in the darkness, and I have knelt there ashamed!

It is a feeble atonement; I know you would not understand these things if I told them to you during your waking hours. But tomorrow I will be a real daddy! I will chum with you, and suffer when you suffer, and laugh when you laugh. I will bite my tongue when impatient words come. I will keep saying as if it were a ritual: "He is nothing but a boy—a little boy!"

I am afraid I have visualized you as a man. Yet as I see you now, son, crumpled and weary in your cot, I see that you are still a baby. Yesterday you were in your mother's arms, your head on her shoulder. I have asked too much, too much.[8]

From an eternal prospective worldly comforts and material things such as boats, campers, vacations, and large, fancy homes, or even college degrees are indeed poor substitutes for neglecting these little angels of heaven. Financially speaking, it is the equivalent of surrendering diamonds for dust.

First and foremost, parents have a sacred obligation to teach their children the ways of the Lord and the importance of walking uprightly before Him. Children must be taught basic gospel principles by parents who actively live them. For, "a child learns more by imitation than in any other way. . . . And the persons he imitates most blindly and trustingly are bound to be his parents. Nature has made the relationship between parent and child such that beside it any other training bears a certain artificiality."[9]

Whether or not it is an oversight of parents or a deficiency in the public school system, one thing is clear, our children are not being taught how to effectively work or manage money. The deficiency is catastrophic. If we fail to teach our children industry and monetary discipline, what hope do they have for a bright future? In a very real sense, haven't we crippled them? Unfortunately, this failure can come full circle and haunt parents by robbing them of retirement funds used to bail out adult children who cannot make their own way or stay out of debt.

Isn't it more important to give children the necessary building blocks to construct a sound future, than to merely fill heads with dates and places? Few things could be more important for today's high school graduates than the ability to attack a task and effectively manage money.

As mentioned earlier, our young people have been subjected to an endless onslaught of clever conditioning that has clouded their sense of financial responsibility. They have been programmed to blindly pursue instant gratification. Unlike any other generation in history, this generation has been raised with the philosophy everything is instant. If you want dinner, just throw something in the microwave and wait a few moments. Pizza anyone? Make a call and several minutes later it is delivered to your doorstep. Need to talk to a friend in Europe? Just dial a few numbers. If mom and dad want new wheels, they need only to apply for another loan and a new car magically appears in the driveway. In young and inexperienced eyes, nothing requires careful planning and saving.

But when the time arrives for these "microwave kids" to strike out on their own, many will join that fast growing sector of the debt-ridden in our society. The allure of what they want and what they think they deserve is readily available. They haven't been taught to prioritize and exercise delayed gratification. Unlike past generations, microwave kids have grown up thinking debt is a normal way to acquire what they want.

When I was well into my teenage years, my father was struggling to help me fulfill one of my church responsibilities—I don't remember what—when the conversation between us turned heated. To father's great shock, these words found their way out of my mouth, "You've had sixteen years to teach me what you wanted me to know. It's over now, you'd better pray you took the time and did it right!" More than sassy words from an ignorant little redhead, my father later recounted the startling realization that I was probably right. Children need to be taught responsibility and hard work as early as possible. President Kimball taught, "Children should learn to work. Parents should not spend their nights and days trying to find something to interest their children. They should find something to occupy them and get them busy doing something that is worthwhile."

Parents often wait until children are teenagers before instructing them about money. My oldest boy was about five or six years old when we decided to take the family to Disneyland. During the weeks preceding the trip, we had Andrew earn spending money by completing odd jobs around the house. He was excited about the trip and worked hard. Before it was time to go, he had earned several dollars. Even at six years old, he knew something about the value of a dollar. Nevertheless, we had scarcely walked through the park gates when Andrew spotted a concession stand and wanted something to eat. As an alternative, we offered him any one of the various snacks that we brought along. But he stubbornly fixated on a small three-dollar box of popcorn.

To teach him this important lesson, we allowed him to spend almost half his personal money on a box of popcorn that was really only worth pennies. It was his money and that's what he wanted to do with it.

A short while later, after the popcorn was gone, Andrew spoke reflectively, "Boy, that was a lot of work for just popcorn." We had extra money we could have given him, but that would have reinforced a negative message, one that might have haunted us for years to come. Andrew needed to understand that money does not perpetually grow on trees. In addition, he needed to connect the dots and learn that each shiny coin has an intrinsic value attached to it. As the proverb goes, give a child a fish and he only has a meal, but teach a child to fish and he will never starve. Again, we want to guard against raising dependent children. One of the greatest blessings we can give our children is the ability to stand and survive on their own.

My father didn't believe in wasting anything. On one occasion, rather than throwing away several hundred pounds of contaminated wheat, my father had us children meticulously sort through each bag and then hand grind the wheat into flour. With the exception of getting to eat the bread, I don't remember being reimbursed for the effort. We understood that it fell under the umbrella of "family survival." Furthermore, I don't remember ever being handed money. If I had a dollar in my pocket it was because I had exchanged time and effort for it. At quite an early age I understood the value of a penny. As Brigham Young said, "Never consider that you have bread enough around you to suffer your children to waste a crust or a crumb of it. If a man is worth millions of bushels of wheat and corn, he is not wealthy enough to suffer his servant girl to sweep a single kernel of it into the fire; let it be eaten by something and pass again into the earth, and thus fulfill the purpose for which it grew. Remember it, do not waste anything, but take care of everything."[11]

One day, my five-year-old daughter Mersadie was at a department store with her mother, and, as some children will do, she asked for everything that caught her eye. Preoccupied, my wife shook her head and said, "No, dear, we don't have the money to buy that today." Exasperated, my daughter blurted out, "Momma, I love Daddy but he doesn't earn nearly enough money for us." My wife then took the opportunity to explain to Mersadie that few people have enough money to buy everything their hearts desire. She further explained that Daddy was working as hard as he could, and if she wanted these things badly enough, perhaps she could think of ways to earn the money. Later, my wife asked Mersadie if she wanted those things more than she wanted her father to be at home in the evenings. The little girl didn't hesitate with her answer. She wanted her father home as often as possible.

Although we desire our children to be obedient, we should carefully guard against ruling them with an iron fist. What we really want is thoughtful and willing obedience, not begrudged or forced compliance. Occasionally, when the conditions are right, children should be allowed to question decisions and exercise guided independence. Let them use their heads as much as possible. A child who is a bit feisty and not completely submissive can be a good thing.

Joseph Joubert said, "Children have more need of models than of critics."[12] Dog handlers apply this idea by utilizing what they call the five-to-one formula. This simply means that dog handlers have discovered that a puppy in training needs a ratio of five positive reinforcements to each negative or corrective reinforcement. Too many positive, and not enough corrective reinforcements, and the puppy becomes unruly and undisciplined. Too many corrective, and not enough positive reinforcements, and the puppy becomes soft and timid.

Children are like puppies. We must diligently teach children correct principles, exercise positive belief in them and then nourish them with plenty of positive reinforcement. Of course we need to exercise caution, but unless there is reason to believe otherwise, trust in what they tell you and let them know how much you value this trust. As they respond, give them special privileges and greater responsibilities. Let them know what kind of greatness you see in them and what kind of child you daily pray they will become. Commenting on her well-adjusted children, a great church leader's wife once remarked she would tell her children yes as often as the situation would allow for it.

As children mature and exercise good judgment, cautiously meter additional freedoms and privileges. They will respond positively instead of being consumed with resentment. "Parents have a duty to govern their children, but the object of all good government is to prepare the subject for self government."[13]

To lead, a child must govern. I vividly remember the first check I received from my early morning paper route. I had a goal to put my money in a bank account and save it for a ten-speed bicycle. Instead, I promptly took my wad of cash to the local grocery store and spent it on a sack full of candy bars. With my sack of treasures in hand, I went home, sequestered myself in my room, poured the sack out on my bed and proceeded to eat the candy bars one at a time. I was in heaven. After a dozen or so I started to feel nauseous; and after about twenty I became extremely ill.

Do I even need to mention that I never made that mistake again? I was completely cured and got that foolishness out of my head forever. I could now move on with my goals. I was more resolved. I came to realize over-indulgences were irresponsible, and every cause has an effect. As a result, I deposited my next paycheck into my savings account. Several months later I had enough to purchase a shiny new Nishiki ten-speed. What a simple yet profound lesson to learn at such a tender age! I then went on to save for other things, including my mission. Children need opportunities to earn money as well as opportunities to spend and govern it. Before they leave home, children should clearly understand that "God sells us things at the price of labor."[14]

Although it seems a bit harsh, children need to be taught there are no free lunches and that money doesn't grow on trees. For this reason I struggle with the widespread practice of giving children free allowances. I personally prefer to have my children earn money by working at odd jobs above and beyond their normal household duties. Some experts strongly disagree with me. They trumpet the value of providing children with weekly allowances and rattle off a long list of advantages. But the bottom line is this: free allowances do not teach children the value of money. Marvin J. Ashton wrote the following: "One of the greatest favors parents can do for their children is to teach them to work. Much has been said over the years about children and monthly allowances, and opinions and recommendations vary greatly. I'm from the 'old school.' I believe children should earn their money needs through service and appropriate chores. . . . I think it is unfortunate for a child to grow up in a home where the seed is planted in the child's mind that there is a family money tree that automatically produces cash once a week or once a month."[15]

Parents should teach children that there are consequences that relate to wise and foolish financial choices. When children want something, show them different ways to earn the money to obtain it. Maybe they could create something as simple as a lemonade stand or bake and sell cookies. Older children have many more opportunities to make money. They can tend younger children, mow lawns, paint fences or sell products and services.

As the song says, "Is this the little girl I carried, Is this the little boy at play? I don't remember growing older—when did they? . . . Sunrise, Sunset—Swiftly fly the years. One season following another, Laden with happiness and tears."[16] And altogether too soon they, as well as the magical influence we had upon them, are gone. Although tired and resting, Jesus, the creator of the universe, cleared His calendar and arranged His busy schedule to love and nurture the little ones, who, in essence, would be gone tomorrow. He did not put them off for a more convenient day—no, not even for a more convenient moment.

The most knowledgeable and powerful being in all eternity has made known His recipe for true and lasting treasure and happiness, "For behold, this is my work and glory to bring to pass the immortality and eternal life of man" (Moses 1:39). It seems incomprehensible that God's work and glory is relegated to the service and development of mankind. Yet it is true according to his own words. And because of this, children are the nursery crop of His entire plan. This is why the Lord is so protective of them—because they eventually become adults. If, first, we have our children and then see to it they are nurtured and taught properly in time, they become righteous men and women and move closer to His goal of immortality and eternal life. If not, He loses them. Therefore, solid, functioning family units are key in this heavenly effort and nothing can compensate for its failure. Nothing! We must ask ourselves then, if this is the goal of the Almighty, Himself, and our fondest aspiration is to eventually follow in His footsteps, to do the things we see our Father do, can we afford to be diverted from our children and family by the tempting allure of this world's treasures?

Where humanly possible, let us prioritize our time and even reduce our lifestyles, if necessary, so mothers can return to one of the most important duties under heaven—raising and nurturing children. Wise are the parents who understand that this is where the real gold is found. Like the mining town for Frisco, everything else crumbles in the shifting sand of time. For the hand that rocks the cradle truly partners with God in shaping the destiny of mankind. The loud and convincing cries from the world will never alter this truth.

Much like he did for the Nephites, may the God of heaven send us a thunderous awakening that we may have the wisdom to stop all this nonsense and seize the moment with our children. For they "are the heritage of the Lord" (Psalm 127:3), and should be our priority and the recipient of our supreme efforts. "Happy is the man that hath his quiver full of them" (Psalm 127:5).

With a heightened degree of urgency, may we hold our children and grandchildren close to us and love them like there is no tomorrow. May we follow the example of our Lord and make time for them today. May we absorb from our children all that is needed to reach our final destination: the exercise of simple faith; contentment with the simple things; and an attitude that is teachable, loving, and forgiving.

It has been aptly stated, "The most important thing a father can do for his children is to love their mother."[17] Equally, the most important thing a mother can do for her children is to love their father. In so doing there will be treasure, power, and splendor beyond anything money can buy.

Speaking of children and the accumulation of wealth, Socrates wrote, "Could I climb to the highest place in Athens, I would lift up my voice and proclaim, 'Fellow citizens, why do ye turn and scrape every stone to gather wealth and take so little care of your children to whom one day you must relinquish it all?' "[18]

Wealth would have us know what God understands, and what the twentieth amazing treasure reiterates:

Next to eternal life, the most precious gift that our Father in Heaven can bestow upon man is His children. Why? Because "The future of the race [and eternity] marches forward on the feet of little children."[19] Oh, the redeeming value of reaching beyond our self-centered tendencies to forego worldly accolades and spotlights for a season and quietly go about shaping the lives of our children. As we do our children right by the Lord and anxiously engage in this holy cause by losing ourselves in their service, they will not only heal our souls here, but they will send us heaven-bound and in the end be our salvation.

Hence, "It's good to have money and the things that money can buy, but it's good too, to check once in a while and make sure you haven't lost the things that money can't buy."[20]

Notes

1. Charles M. Dickinson, The Children, "Charles M. Dickinson Quotes," http://www.worldofquotes.com/author/Charles-M.-Dickinson/l/index.html
2. Edward Gibbon, *Decline and Fall of the Roman Empire,* 2nd ed. (London: John Murray, 1846).
3. M. Russell Ballard, "The Sacred Responsibilities of Parenthood," *Ensign*, Mar. 2006, 26–33.
4. Phillips Brooks, *The Light of the World* (Boston: E.P. Dutton and company, 1891), 105.
5. G.K. Chesterson, *What's Wrong with the World* (Ft. Collins, CO: Ignatius Press, 1994), 155.
6. *The Family: A Proclamation to the World* (Salt Lake City: Intellectual Reserve, 1995).
7. "The Father and the Home," *Improvement Era,* June 1958, 410; quoting from Samuel S. Leibowitz, "Nine Words That Can Stop Juvenile Delinquency," *Reader's Digest*, Mar. 1958, 106.
8. W. Livingston Larned, "Father Forgets" (as quoted in *Reader's Digest*), www.mansinnerjourney.com/documents/FatherForgets.pdf.
9. "George Sanderlin quote," http://www.hort.wisc.edu/cran/pubs_archive/newsletters/2004/news_2004_05_20.html.
10. Spencer W. Kimball, "Family Preparedness," *Ensign*, May 1976, 124.
11. Brigham Young, "Use and Abuse of Blessings," *Journal of Discourses,* vol. 1 (accessed Jan. 9, 2009: http://en.wikisource.org/wiki/Journal_of_Discourses/Volume_1/Use_and_Abuse_of_Blessings).
12. "Joseph Joubert quotes," http://en.wikiquote.org/wiki/Joseph_Joubert.

13. Dr. Lyman Abbot in *Richard Evans' Quote Book* (Salt Lake City: Publishers Press, 1971), 183.
14. Leonardo da Vinci, "Quotations about Labor," http://www.quotegarden.com/labor.html.
15. Marvin J. Ashton, "Guide to Family Finance," Liahona, Apr. 2000, 42.
16. Sheldon Harnick, "Sunrise, Sunset," http://www.ne.jp/asahi/minako/watanabe/suneng.htm.
17. Author Unknown in *Richard Evans' Quote Book* (Salt Lake City: Publishers Press, 1971).
18. Socrates in *Richard Evans' Quote Book* (Salt Lake City: Publishers Press, 1971).
19. Phillips Brooks in *Richard Evans' Quote Book* (Salt Lake City: Publishers Press, 1971), 32.
20. "Quotes by George Horace Lorimer in Money category," http://www.quoteworld.org/category/money/author/george_horace_lorimer.

"There is no regularly constituted church on the earth, nor any person authorized to administer any church ordinances; nor can there be until new apostles are sent by the Great Head of the Church for whose coming I am seeking." —Colonial American, Roger Williams[1]

Amazing Treasure Number Twenty-one

The Restoration: Salvation from Heaven

Archimedes once boldly proclaimed, "Had we a place to stand upon, we might raise the world."[2] With such an audacious declaration the question begs to be asked, where does such a foundation exists for which to plant our feet?

Several hundred years before the long awaited birth in Bethlehem of Judea, Isaiah, the most quoted of all Christian prophets, foretold of a mighty work that would commence in the latter days. Looking down through the annals of time, with crude ink and quill, Isaiah boldly prophesied,

> Wherefore the Lord said, Forasmuch as this people draw near me with their mouth, and with their lips do honour me, but have removed their heart far from me, and their fear toward me is taught by the precept of men: Therefore, behold, I will proceed to do a marvelous work among this people, even a marvelous work and a wonder: for the wisdom of their wise men shall perish, and the understanding of their prudent man shall be hid. . . . And in that day shall the deaf hear the words of the book [Book of Mormon], and the eyes of the blind shall see out of obscurity, and out of darkness. (Isaiah 29:13-14, 18)

Hence, a heavenly treasure begins to unfold in the latter days.

Deep in the recesses of my memory is a story so moving and beautiful I have concluded it must must have been a dream. I have recorded this profound event entitled "The Morning Breaks" thusly:

It was so early in the morning; it was still dark outside. I was busy assisting the prophet and his wife with their luggage downstairs to an awaiting vehicle. His wife seemed tired, and I felt sorry that she had to get up at such an unearthly hour. Despite how she felt, she labored dutifully to put one foot in front of the other as we made our way to the garage. He always appeared more energetic than his sweet little wife—it was as though he was running on energy from another sphere. He was a man on a mission! Within his soul burned an urgency to bare his special witness to the four corners of earth. I was privileged on numerous occasions to witness his powerful prophetic testimony, and it moved me to the core every time.

How different their lives were from ordinary people. No rocking chairs or motor-homes. As a private, unassuming couple I'm certain they struggled with the notoriety of their position, in addition to a distressing awareness that their lives would never be their own again.

The next ten days would be grueling for this couple well into their eighties. Their son, daughter-in-law, and the prophet's personal secretary were waiting in the garage. Soon, the luggage was packed in the trunk. After assisting them into the car, we headed toward the airport.

My heart thrilled as I contemplated the larger picture. Looking back on history it was obvious times had changed for the Latter-day Saint people. No longer were they a small, scrubby band of persecuted Saints desperately trying to find a home to practice their new beliefs and live in peace. To escape bitter persecution they fled to an unwanted, isolated desert, and it soon blossomed as a rose. Many Saints died along the prairie en route to their new Zion. Witnessing this migration lead Isaiah to extol, "The wilderness and the solitary place shall be glad for them; and the desert shall rejoice, and blossom as the rose" (Isaiah 35:1). Today, for the most part, they are a respected, well-established people numbering into the millions. Their numbers grow daily with a force of over fifty-thousand missionaries serving throughout the world. LDS chapels and stake centers cover not only the American continent, but many of the continents of the earth. Our temples now dot the globe. Beyond question, we have become a powerful and influential people. We are held synonymously with such virtues as honesty, industry, and hard work. We are respected and enjoy positions of responsibility in both government and in the corporate world.

The stone spoken of by the Old Testament prophet Daniel has not only been cut out of the mountain but is rolling forth with great momentum as it fulfills its final destination. "Thou sawest till that a stone was cut out without hands. . . . And in the days of these kings shall the God of heaven set up a kingdom, which shall never be destroyed: and the kingdom shall not be left to other people, but it shall break in pieces and consume all these kingdoms, and it shall stand for ever" (Daniel 2:34, 44).

I thought back to the beginning when the stone was first cut. To most of the earth's inhabitants, the day was rather ordinary. And while the exact date is uncertain, we know it was in early spring. Although the special occasion was void of the pomp and ceremony that typically accompany major world events, it proved to be a day that would go down in history books. World governments and religious leaders of the day were preoccupied with matters of church and state. Yet it was of little consequence, as none were invited. This was to be a heavenly event. Consequently, there were no uniformed armies marching for royal review; no fireworks bursting in darkened skies; no red carpet celebrations in castles and capitals across distant nations, no pageantry. However, with so much at stake, there were also no mere angels dispatched from heaven, for this message was to be personally delivered by the Father and the Son.

Satan was present, even if for a brief moment; and though the world lay in a haze of ignorance, he fully understood the significance of the occasion. The event would prove to be a great disturbance to his kingdom, and he cleverly set out to prevent it. The advent of this grand, unprecedented theophany marked a limit to Satan's days, and, true to his character, he would not go without a fight. He knew where, when, and whom to attack. Despite his cunning efforts to prevent this event, Satan could not prevail, for young Joseph later declared, "I saw a pillar of light exactly over my head, above the brightness of the sun, which descended gradually until it fell upon me. It no sooner appeared than I found myself delivered from the enemy which held me bound." (Joseph Smith History 1:16-17). Even with heaven's intervention, Satan would prove tenacious and unrelenting. From the grove to Carthage, he would never let Joseph enjoy another moment of peace. Satan and his nefarious forces tormented him at every turn and at every climb.

Most importantly, though, on that very day the most significant episode since the death and resurrection of the Savior began to unfold quietly in a grove of trees in upper state New York, where God, Himself, and His

Son Jesus Christ descended from Their heavenly thrones and personally appeared to a poor, unlearned farm boy to reveal unto him glorious news from heaven—that soon the Kingdom of God would again be established upon the earth. Young Joseph triumphantly declared, For "I had actually seen a light, and in the midst of that light I saw two Personages, and they did in reality speak to me; and though I was hated and persecuted for saying that I had seen a vision, yet it was true. . . . I knew it and I knew God knew it, and I could not deny it, neither dared I do it; at least I knew that by so doing I would offend God, and come under condemnation" (Joseph Smith History 1:25). Although earth lay in a haze of ignorance, I imagine numberless trumpets from the far corners of heaven announced the long-awaited circumstances.

An ancient record emerged and finally spoke from the dust as prophesied. It was boldly presented to the world as sacred scripture. Witnesses were summoned and established as hell's darkness and diabolical fury bore down on this seemingly insignificant movement. Though each of the three witnesses fell out of favor with the young prophet and became personal enemies, they would tenaciously honor their testimonies of the Book of Mormon to their graves: While two of the witnesses eventually returned, one remained estranged to the end. In spite of all this they solemnly affirmed together,

> Be it known unto all nations, kindreds, tongues, and people, unto whom this work shall come: That we, through the grace of God the Father, and our Lord Jesus Christ, have seen the plates which contain this record. . . . And we declare with words of soberness, that an angel of God came down from heaven, and he brought and laid before our eyes, that we beheld and saw the plates, and the engravings thereon. . . . It is marvelous in our eyes. Nevertheless, the voice of the Lord commanded us that we should bear record of it[3]

I pondered the lowly farmer's futile attempt to gain redress for his wronged people from the leaders in the nation's capitol and how his message fell on deaf ears. I thought of the contrast today and how I had personally witnessed United States presidents, government leaders, and world royalty and dignitaries come from distant lands to Salt Lake City to visit with the LDS leadership. I thought of the millions and millions of people who travel from the far corners of earth to visit Temple Square and church headquarters. "And it shall come to pass in the last days, that the mountain of the Lord's house shall be established in the top of the mountains, and shall be exalted above the hills; and all nations shall flow unto it" (Isaiah 2:2).

At thirty-nine years old, knowing the fate that imminently awaited him, Joseph reflected, "I am going like a lamb to the slaughter, but I am calm as a summer's morning, I have a conscience void of offense toward God and toward men" (D&C 135:4). Three days later, Joseph would pay the ultimate price for his work and testimony. "And now, after the many testimonies which have been given of him, this is the testimony, last of all, which we give of him: That he lives! For we saw him, even on the right hand of God; and we heard the voice bearing record that he is the Only Begotten of the Father." (D&C 76:22–23)

We drove through the huge hangar and onto the tarmac, where I pulled along the side of the sleek jet. I assisted them out of the car and then began to unload the luggage from the car to the aircraft. It seemed as though everyone took a moment to gaze in awe at the beautiful twenty-first century wonder. The jet engines were warming and the navigational lights illuminated the predawn hour.

I considered that it would have taken President Brigham Young about the same amount of time to make a round trip to southern Utah as it would for this President to complete a several-nation tour. Brigham would have met with hundreds of Saints, while this President would meet with hundreds of thousands. Even until recently, the Presidents were relegated to flying the cumbersome commercial airlines, which made such a multinational tour far more complex, time consuming and virtually impossible, given their elderly ages. Times were undeniably changing.

Soon, the party boarded the plane and the hydraulic door slowly retracted. As the sunlight crested the eastern Rocky Mountains a chill shot from the top of my head to the bottom of my toes. I watched the morning's first rays of soft light slowly chase away the remnants of night. It seemed symbolic of the first song in our hymnal: "The Morning Breaks."

> The morning breaks, the shadows flee; Lo, Zion's standard is unfurled; The dawning of a brighter day majestic rises on the world.
>
> The clouds of error disappear Before the rays of truth divine; The Glory bursting from afar wide o'er the nations soon will shine. . . .
>
> Jehovah speaks! Let earth give ear, And Gentile nations turn and live. His mighty arm is making bare His covenant to receive.
>
> Angels from Heav'n and truth from earth have met, and both have

> record borne; Thus Zion's light is bursting forth, to bring her ransomed children home.[4]

As sunlight burst from over the horizon, and the jet taxied to the runway to await instructions from the tower, engines roared, and soon the amazing bird was a distant dot high in the earth's atmosphere and was moving at a super-speed toward its distant destinations. On board was a prophet of God to bless and teach the nations. Like the restoration, shadows of ignorance and sin will flee his presence and a glorious light will fill the void. For it is written in the Preface to the Doctrine and Covenants:

> Hearken, O ye people of my church, saith the voice of him who dwells on high, and whose eyes are upon all men; yea, verily I say: Hearken ye people from afar; and ye that are upon the islands of the sea, listen together.
>
> For verily the voice of the Lord is unto all men, and there is none to escape; and there is no eye that shall not see, neither ear that shall not hear, neither heart that shall not be penetrated. . . .
>
> And they [the prophet and the Quorum of the Twelve Apostles] shall go forth and none shall stay them, for I the Lord have commanded them.
>
> Behold, this is mine authority, and the authority of my servants . . . which I have given them.

Again my mind drifted. Referencing the apostasy, the resulting dark ages it brought upon the earth, and the long awaited restitution of His gospel,

> Jesus answered and said unto them, Take heed that no man deceive you. For many shall come in my name, saying, I am Christ; and shall deceive many. And ye shall hear of wars and rumours of wars: see that ye be not troubled: for all these things must come to pass, but the end is not yet. For nation shall rise against nation, and kingdom against kingdom: and there shall be famines, and pestilences, and earthquakes, in divers places. All these are the beginning of sorrows. . . . And many false prophets shall rise, and shall deceive many. And because iniquity shall abound, the love of many shall wax cold. But he that shall endure unto the end, the same shall be saved. And [then, after all these things have come to pass] this gospel of the kingdom shall be preached in all the world for a witness unto all nations; and then shall the end come." (Matthew 24:4–8, 11–14)

God the Father and His son Jesus Christ have revealed themselves and spoken to us in our day. The bestowal of priesthood keys by heavenly messengers followed the first vision. We live in a glorious day and time when the great angel Moroni has taken flight and delivered the stick of Joseph to be joined in one hand with the stick of Judah (Ezekiel 37:16–17). Together they stand as a mighty ensign to a divided world, a convincing irrefutable witness of the truthfulness of the restoration and the divinity of Jesus Christ. "And I saw another angel fly in the midst of heaven, having the everlasting gospel to preach unto them that dwell on the earth, and to every nation, and kindred, and tongue, and people" (Revelation 14:6).

Notwithstanding the sinister mobs conspiring, with his days numbered and entrusted to God, despised by many and honored by few, Joseph valiantly declared, "No unhallowed hand can stop the work from progressing; persecutions may rage, mobs may combine, armies may assemble, calumny may defame, but the truth of God will go forth boldly. Nobly and independent, till it has penetrated every continent; visited every clime, swept every country, and sounded in every ear; till the purposes of God shall be accomplished, and the great Jehovah shall say the work is done."[5]

Due to the apostasy that was to shortly follow his departure, Jesus offered a simple yet profound way to identify his people, "Wherefore by their fruits ye shall know them" (Matthew 7:20). The very presence of apostles and prophets on the earth today is a sign that marks the advent of "a marvelous work and a wonder" brought about by God's own hand. For after much darkness and chaos, the heavens have once again revealed themselves to mankind, and the kingdom of God has been reestablished upon the face of the earth.

A bit choked up and with my heart overflowing, I put the car in gear and headed back to Salt Lake City. Neither Isaiah, nor Daniel, nor John the Revelator had anything up on me. All of them would have given anything to see what I had just witnessed.

Years have passed since these awe-inspiring images were imprinted upon my memory, and I have at times reflected on my own personal encounters with the power of Joseph Smith, the Restoration, and the Book of Mormon.

In 1981, baptisms across my mission had been steadily falling for months, which greatly concerned the mission president. Out of desperation, he sent my companion and me out on a fact-finding assignment.

After touring and working with missionaries throughout the mission for a couple of weeks, we returned with our answer. The name Joseph Smith was unpopular in the South, and to avoid confrontation the missionaries had slowly excluded discussion of the falling away and Restoration as well as the bearing of any testimony of Joseph Smith. "He called me by name, and said unto me that he was a messenger sent from the presence of God to me, and that his name was Moroni; that God had a work for me to do; and that my name should be had for good and evil among all nations, kindreds, and tongues, or that it should be both good and evil spoken of among all people" (Joseph Smith History 1:33).

A conference was promptly convened; our mission president stood before those young missionaries and bore a powerful testimony of Joseph Smith and the Restoration. He said that neither could be excluded for true conversion. Almost immediately, baptisms began to rise.

On another occasion, a little over halfway through this mission, my good friend Oliver Davis approached me and my companion and informed us of a family who had accepted his offer to be taught the gospel. Mr. Shelton had recently retired, and his wife was an accomplished school teacher. They had three children still living at home when we met them in 1980.

After about the third discussion, Mrs. Shelton and the children were actively reading the Book of Mormon and had already developed tender testimonies. Mr. Shelton on the other hand was growing more and more guarded and aloof—so unlike when we first met him. He wasn't progressing, and we worried we would lose him and possibly cause a division in this otherwise amazing family. He had a lot of questions and was filled with doubt.

During our last visit we bore powerful testimonies of the authenticity of the Book of Mormon. We challenged him again to read and pray about its truthfulness and explained that the Book of Mormon was the very keystone to our religion; if it were true, our message was the most important message on earth; if it were false, we were indeed imposters. He accepted the challenge. The family also positively received our offer to work toward a baptismal date two weeks away and agreed to come to church. They had agreed to come the week before, but never showed. When Sunday rolled around, to our continued disappointment, the Sheltons were not at church. Before leaving the chapel we were informed that Mr. Shelton had been rushed to the hospital with serious symptoms and that the family was requesting a blessing from the missionaries.

As I laid my hands on his head to seal the anointing, I was moved to promise him that by the Lord's priesthood and power he would be healed, but that the blessing was predicated upon following what he knew in his heart to be true. In fact, he was promised that he would be healed in time to make his baptismal date the following week. This sudden illness had been a frightening and emotional ordeal for the entire family. I could see the relief in their faces when the blessing concluded.

Before leaving, Brother Shelton invited me and my companion to have a seat as he had something special to tell us. Apparently, instead of coming to our church the week before, he had taken his family to his church to pray for guidance. During the service the minister invited those who were interested to come to the altar to pray. Brother Shelton responded, and as he knelt at the altar he put his hands over his eyes and silently pleaded for direction from the Lord. This had been his family's church for many years. He had served in leadership roles, and his family had been taught and had worshiped within its walls. He knew and loved these people and did not want to hurt or abandon them. He could also feel the division developing within his family.

Yet he also felt pulled by something he did not completely understand. He prayed fervently. Suddenly, with his hands still covering his eyes, he saw a tunnel as plainly as if his eyes were wide open. As he looked down into the opening, he could see a box constructed of slabs of stone; inside the box he could clearly see the golden plates as we had described them a few weeks earlier.

He said in an emotional voice, "Elders, there I was at the altar of my church, praying about the truthfulness of the Book of Mormon when this vision of the keystone to your religion opened up before me. I've known it was true ever since, but was unwilling to commit to it at the time." We challenged him to take the leap of faith and be baptized next week. He readily accepted. "And it shall come to pass in the last days, saith God, I will pour out of my Spirit upon all flesh: and your sons and your daughters shall prophesy, and your young men shall see visions, and your old men shall dream dreams. . . . And I will shew wonders in heaven above, and signs in the earth beneath; blood, and fire, and vapour of smoke" (Acts 2:17, 19).

Before we left him that day we learned that his condition could be serious—he had even had a close relative die recently and the doctors were worried that Brother Shelton might be suffering from the same illness.

Notwithstanding, a few days later, with the tests in, he was released with a clean bill of health. The family was baptized the following Sunday.

This profound answer to humble prayer served as an anchor to this family. In spite of their fears and hardships, they carved out a legacy for themselves by aligning their lives with the word of the Lord. They have served in positions of service and responsibility in His vineyard throughout the years and have remained "steadfast and immovable" in the testimony of the truth.

The Book of Mormon contains a wonderful and remarkable spirit. Joseph Smith declared the Book of Mormon to be "the most correct book," and stated that a person "would get nearer to God by abiding its percepts than by any other book."[6] Moreover, the Book of Mormon and Bible testify of each other and stand as powerful witnesses of the divinity of Jesus Christ. "And we talk of Christ, we rejoice in Christ, we preach of Christ, we prophesy of Christ, and we write according to our prophecies, that our children may know to what source they may look for a remission of their sins" (2 Nephi 25:26).

Side by side, these two canonical texts of scripture stand as a witnesses to the inhabitants of the earth of the kingdom of God. Together they reaffirm that "straight is the gate and narrow is the way to salvation and eternal life." The morning light of truth has broken through, and the shadow of ignorance has been lifted. Surely this is wealth and treasure beyond all description!

To all who may read these words, I bear record that The Church of Jesus Christ of Latter-Day Saints is indeed the place to stand if the world is to be elevated. In our day there truly exists a foundation laid by the hand of God that is the source of salvation for mankind.

As with the sublime supremacy of heavenly choirs, the twenty-first amazing treasure proclaims this celestial truth:

One could deplete the fertile mine fields of earth and not find the treasure to be had in a single word sent from God. Imagine then the wealth of he who possesses all of His word necessary for salvation and eternal life. Yet heavenly truths have been restored upon the earth today and mankind will discover priceless treasures as well as eternal joy in its fervent pursuit. Oh, inhabitants of the earth fall upon your knees and rejoice for the heavens have been opened and the fullness of the gospel spoken of by the Lord and His ancient prophets has once again been established upon the earth. "And he shall send Jesus Christ which before was preached unto you: Whom the heaven must receive until the times of restitution of all things, which God hath spoken by the mouth of all his holy prophets since the world began" (Acts 3:20–21).

Notes

1. "Roger Williams quotes," http://en.wikipedia.org/wiki/Roger_Williams_(theologian).
2. Archimedes as quoted in *Literary History of the United States: History* (accessed Jan 9, 2009: http://www.archive.org/stream/literaryhistoryo008890mbp/literaryhistoryo008890mbp_djvu.txt).
3. Oliver Cowdery, David Whitmer, and Martin Harris, "The Testimony of Three Witnesses," *Book of Mormon* (Salt Lake City: Intellectual Reserve).
4. Parley P. Pratt, "The Morning Breaks," *Hymns* (Salt Lake City: Intellectual Reserve, 1998), 1.
5. *History of the Church*, vol. 4, 2nd ed. (Salt Lake City: Deseret Book, 1978), 540.
6. *History of the Church*, vol. 4, 2nd ed. (Salt Lake City: Deseret Book, 1978), 461.

"The dogmas of the quiet past are inadequate to the stormy present. The occasion is piled high with difficulty, and we must arise with the occasion. As our case is new, so we must think anew and act anew."
—Abraham Lincoln[1]

Conclusion

When The Dust Settles: The Eternal Perspective

My family has raised chickens for many years. Once you have had fresh eggs you can never go back to store-bought eggs. Red Harry the rooster is a character who once graced our little farm. Red Harry hated to be restricted in any way; he especially hated the limitations of the coop. When my young children would open the door to feed the chickens, Red Harry would make his move, and like a convict dart for the opening. The kids would swat him away or quickly close the door to block his escape. One day Red Harry was successful in breaking free, and the kids could not catch him again.

For the next several days the rest of the chickens lined up inside the pen to watch the coop idol roam about the farm, feeding on greens of every sort, consuming bugs and dirt to his gizzard's content. Soon we had a serious case of Red Harry envy invade the coop. In the eyes of the chickens, Red Harry was completely free. He ate what he wanted when he wanted. One night he would roost high in the trees or atop the coop the next. Unrestrained by mesh walls, he came and went as he pleased and often strutted past the feathered ladies as if to taunt them. Late one night, I was awakened by an awful commotion outside. I jumped out of bed and turned on the exterior lights to survey the farm and coop—all appeared well, and so I retired back to bed.

The next morning I was about my chores and noticed a red ball of feathers a short distance from the coop. It was the bones and feathers of Red Harry. A wild skunk or mink had made easy food of him. He had no chance against such a predator. I also noticed the animal had dug around the coop in several spots but hit buried mesh each time and finally gave up. In my humble opinion, Red Harry didn't die in vain, because if chickens can talk amongst each other, and I swear they do, from that night on there was no more Red Harry envy. It was as though the egg-laying ladies made the connection in that little mass behind their beaks that the coop wasn't there to keep them in nearly as much as it was to keep bad guys out. Like the safety of the coop, these twenty-one time-honored treasures will shield you from unnecessary pain, anguish, and danger.

N. Eldon Tanner put forth a point I wish to close with. He said, "The choice to serve God, worthily made, does not necessarily preclude a home or sufficient money or income, or the things of this world which bring joy and happiness, but it does require that we must not turn away from God and the teachings of Jesus Christ while in the pursuit of our temporal needs."[2]

If I understand President Tanner correctly, we can love and serve God, as well as enjoy the material things of this world, if we keep our priorities straight and do things in the right order.

As previously discussed, money has incredible powers. The love of it can possess us to the point that it destroys us, and the poor use of it can entrap us and bring us misery. If we keep our eternal priorities in perspective and wisely use our money, we can buy time, serve others, and receive rich temporal and eternal blessings. Our homes can and should be a haven from the stains and chaos of this world. They should be nice, neat, and functional. Our resources should be sufficient to provide for our families no matter what the future brings. We should place ourselves in a position to assist the poor and the less fortunate.

Once again, perhaps the wisest counsel comes from the Lord himself, "Seek not for riches but for wisdom; and, behold, the mysteries of God shall be unfolded unto you, and then shall you be made rich. Behold, he that hath eternal life is rich" (D&C 11:7).

I believe the Lord intended His people to be a strong, healthy, independent, honorable, and a generous people, not easily distracted by the applause or glitter of the world. We were created to be free and not enslaved by our passions or the arm of flesh. "Men are that they might have joy" (2 Nephi 2:25). It is my hope and prayer that what I have shared with you will help you attain that joy more abundantly.

I have now done my part by sharing with you these largely forgotten treasures. However, as Richard L. Evans reminds us, "There are some things you can give another person, and some things you cannot give him, except as he is willing to reach out and take them, and pay the price of making them a part of himself. This principle applies to studying, to developing talents, to absorbing knowledge, to acquiring skills, and to the learning of all the lessons of life."[3] The rest is in your hands. It is up to you to act.

And now the questions must be asked, do you possess the courage to break away from the old, self-enslaving habits that will forever hold you earthbound? Do you have the courage to walk beyond the well-lit arena of comfort and crowd, beyond norms and status quo, far above the stratosphere, and step into the never-ending realm of dreams and possibilities?

Richard L. Evans continues, "One of the marks of the executive is the ability to decide. One of the obligations of free men is the willingness to decide. One of the qualities of effective people is the courage to decide."

I challenge you to decide this day how you will live your life henceforth. I challenge you to believe, to act, to reach for the stars, and truly take control of your life. William Shakespeare once penned these words—"Security is mortals' chiefest enemy."[4]

You now possess priceless and powerful knowledge. Wisdom is the wise use of that knowledge. Therefore, be wise, tear off that weighty cocoon; spread your beautiful wings and fly. And remember, "He is rich who owes nothing."

Remember Joseph F. Smith's words: "This knowledge of truth, combined with proper regard for it, and its faithful observance, constitutes true education. The mere stuffing of the mind with a knowledge of facts is not education. The mind must not only possess a knowledge of truth, but the soul must revere it, cherish it, love it as a priceless gem; and this human life must be guided by it in order to fulfill its destiny."[5]

As the great winding-up scenes unfold before us, as the earth reels to and fro on its axes as a drunkard, may we be found loving (D&C 88:87). May God grant people everywhere the uncommon will and foresight to act upon and defend truth whenever or wherever they find it. May God bless us to have the strength and resolve to fight the onslaught of evil and darkness that descends upon us daily, to cling to freedom and the iron rod with unequaled, unwavering tenacity, and to bravely and boldly give our dreams life. And ever, in the face of opposition, see those dreams through to the end and never, never, *never* give up! And wealth will surely follow.

Notes

1. "Abraham Lincoln quote," http://www.quotesandpoem.com/quotes/showquotes/author/Abraham_Lincoln/5512.
2. N. Eldon Tanner, "Choose You This Day," *Ensign*, Jun 1971, 11.
3. Richard L. Evans in *Richard Evans' Quote Book* (Salt Lake City: Publishers Press, 1971), 74.
4. Shakespeare, "Macbeth," Act III, scene 5, http://shakespeare.mit.edu/macbeth/macbeth.3.5.html.
5. Joseph F. Smith as quoted by Royden G. Derrick, " 'By Their Fruits Ye Shall Know Them'," *Ensign*, Nov. 1984, 61.

Acknowledgments

This book has been a lifetime in the making and many people have helped formulate any wisdom contained within its pages. I would like to pay special tribute to my late mission President and his wife, Sloan Alma and Alberta Smith and dedicate my first treasure to this wonderful couple who changed my life. To the late Oliver Davis of Asheville, North Carolina, and to the late John Rich of Jacob Lake, Arizona, for believing in me, for taking the time to care and give me direction at the critical crossroads of my life. Their extraordinary efforts significantly added to the foundation which was laid by my parents and have enriched and blessed my family.

To the brethren of the Church of Jesus Christ of Latter Day Saints whom I have come to know, respect, and deeply love. Each of these men literally wears themselves out in this high and holy calling as the Lord's anointed. Each willingly carries this heavy mantle to their final resting place with their testimonies pronounced to the nations and sealed with a life of service. They are good and upright men, chosen and qualified by the Lord. They are His mouthpieces and special witnesses.

I would like to thank Kate Piersanti of San Pablo, California who believed in this message so completely that she donated many hours of her own time re-editing this message. A stranger at the time, she literally came out of nowhere and took this material to a new and professional level. She was an angel sent to us from heaven.

To my dear parents who never gave up on me and raised this adventurous redhead with the patience of Job, thank you seems entirely inadequate. They sacrificed everything for me and my nine brothers and sisters. I love you, Mom and Dad.

I wish to thank the teachers, mentors, family, and friends, who took the time to encourage and give me direction. I have made you a part of my life. And, although I have moved in the circles of influential people for a large part of my adult life, I have learned the greatest lessons of my life from my beautiful children. I love you, Andrew, Mersadie, Mariah, Cheyenne, Joseph, and Benjamin.

about the author

Jeffrey Hair is a dual citizen of the United States of America and the Great Common Wealth of Australia. He sees himself as a rather ordinary man who had the high honor and privilege of protecting this world's most extraordinary and insightful dignitaries. As fear strikes at the collective populace in these uncertain times, he credits the peace in his life to the adherence of a principle he observed in each of their lives—that "to be rich is to owe nothing." He loves the simple life and enjoys puttering around his little farm in the Salt Lake Valley. He believes his perspective is enhanced when his hands are deep in fertile soil, and his greatest inspiration comes while working on his John Deere tractor. As the proud father of six children, he occasionally reminds them that they are eternally indebted to him for their good looks and sweet dispositions. After all, he was responsible for convincing the sweetest and most beautiful girl under heaven to be their mother.

0 26575 52507 6